BELFAST

STREET & ATLAS GUIDE

CONTENTS

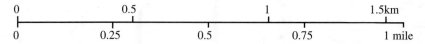

Scale of maps is 1:15,000 (4.2 inches to 1 mile)

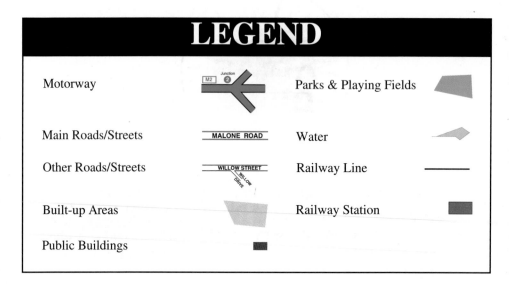

LEGEND

Motorway		Parks & Playing Fields
Main Roads/Streets	MALONE ROAD	Water
Other Roads/Streets	WILLOW STREET / WILLOW DRIVE	Railway Line
Built-up Areas		Railway Station
Public Buildings		

The maps on pages 4 to 28 are based upon the Ordnance Survey of Northern Ireland with the permission of the Controller of Her Majesty's Stationery Office. Crown Copyright reserved. (Permit number 1329).

Printed by The Universities Press (Belfast) Ltd.

Edited by Paul Slevin. Comments, suggestions and inquiries should be addressed to him at the address below. Published by Causeway Press (N.I.), Enterprise House, Balloo Avenue, Bangor, N.Ireland BT19 7QT. Phone (01247) 271 525. Fax (01247) 270 080. E-mail paulslevin@talk21.com

DISTRIBUTION: Distributed by Eason Wholesale Books, 21-25 Boucher Road, Belfast BT12 6QU. Phone 381200 and quote ISBN 1 872600 53 0.

ACKNOWLEDGEMENTS: Photographs by Gerri Slevin. Thanks go to Catherine Coyle, Gerri Slevin, Margaret Coyle, Peter Welsh and Gordon Welsh for their help and research.

BELFAST

STREET ATLAS & GUIDE

We all like to kill two birds with one stone, so to speak, but the Belfast Street Atlas & Guide is that extremely rare bird which offers several different products for the price of one.

Firstly, it is a street atlas of the greater Belfast area, based on the Ordnance Survey. These maps, together with separate rail and bus maps, will help you to navigate your way through and around the city.

Secondly, it is a detailed guide to the best of what Belfast has to offer. Whether you are visiting for the first time or have lived here all your life, our aim is to help you make the most of this increasingly vibrant city as it begins to reap the dividends of the ongoing peace process.

The guide is written and published in Northern Ireland, and is based on contributions from people who have immersed themselves in the Belfast social scene with scant regard to their need of sleep and the health of their livers. Having said that, we are always keen to hear alternative views. If you have any recommendations to make or any contrary views to express regarding any of our choices, please write, fax or e-mail to the addresses given on the page opposite. Any contributions which we use in the future will be acknowledged and a copy of the next edition will be sent in return for the best letters.

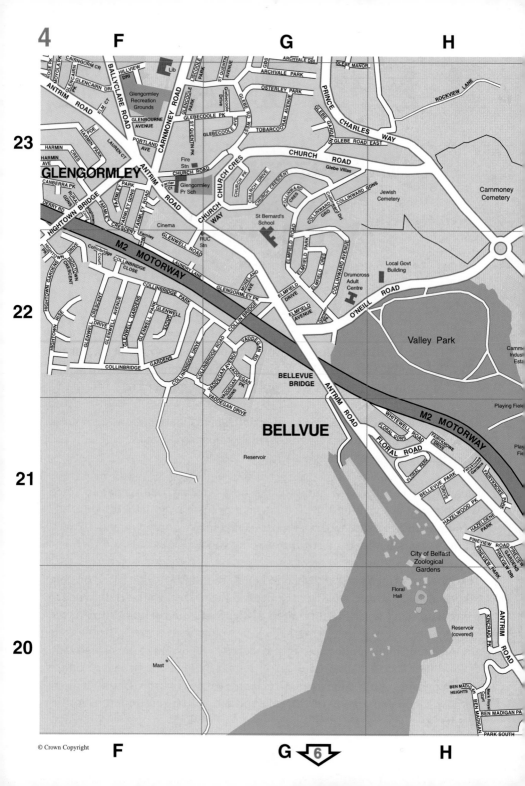

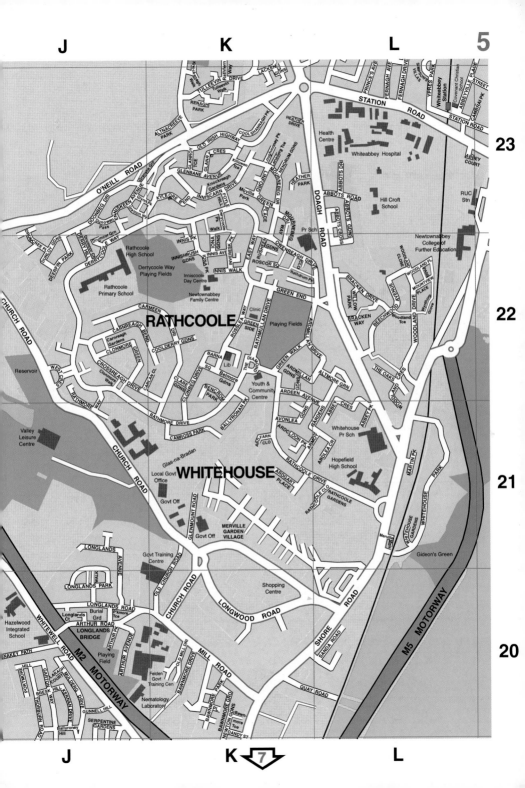

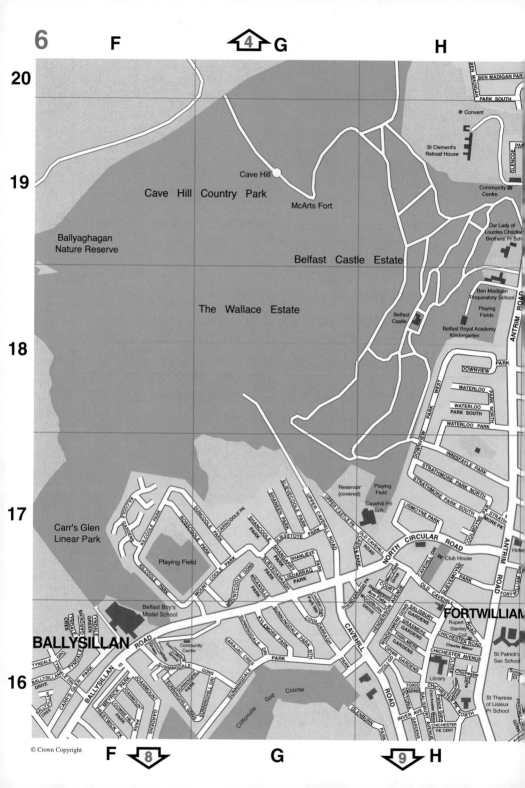

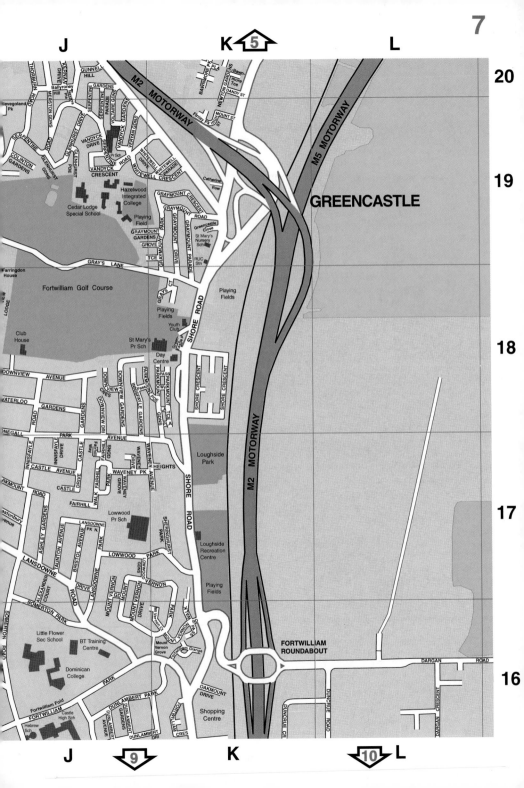

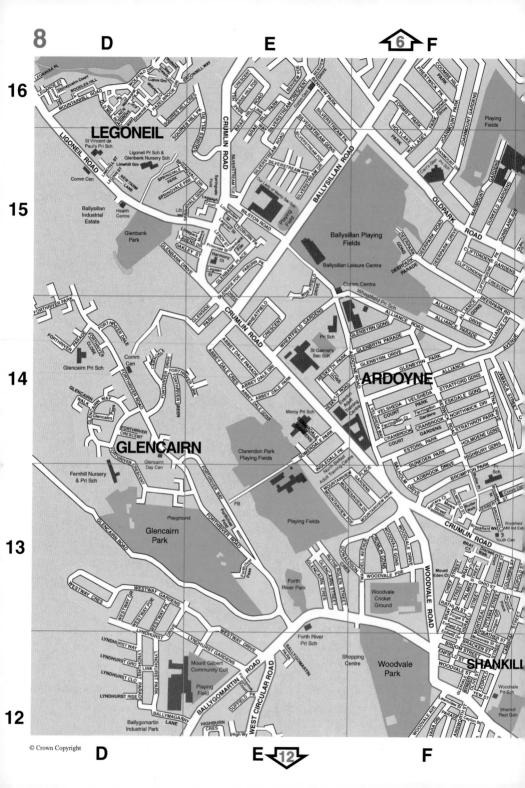

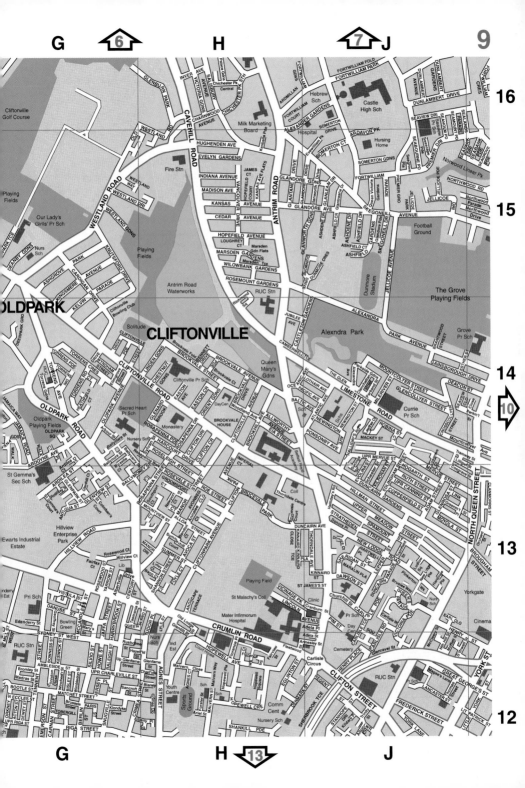

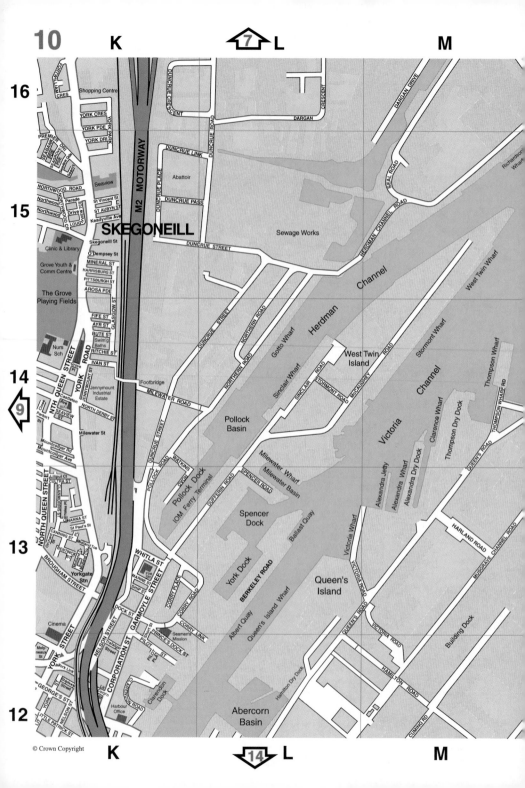

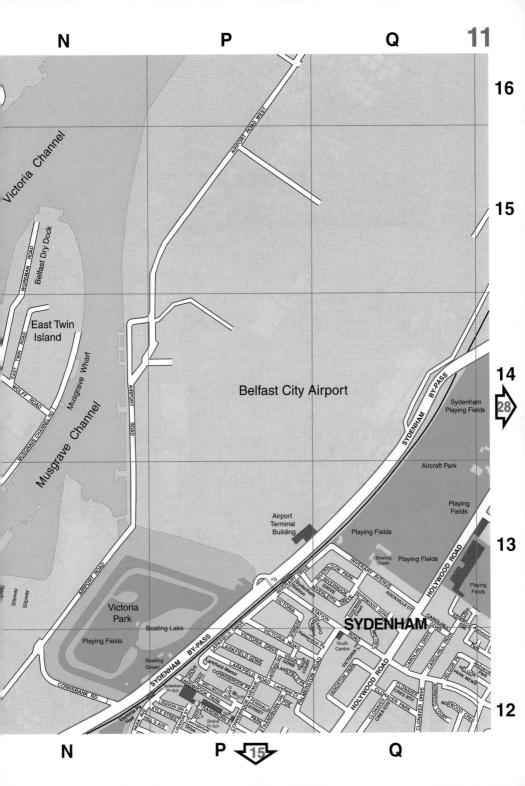

Victoria Channel

Belfast Dry Dock

WORKMAN ROAD

East Twin Island

EAST TWIN ROAD

WOLFF ROAD

MUSGRAVE CHANNEL RD

Musgrave Wharf

Musgrave Channel

AIRPORT ROAD

AIRPORT ROAD WEST

Belfast City Airport

SYDENHAM BY-PASS

Sydenham Playing Fields

Aircraft Park

Playing Fields

Airport Terminal Building

Playing Fields

Playing Fields

HOLYWOOD ROAD

Playing Fields

Bowling Green

INVERARY AVENUE

INVERBROOK PARK

INVERBROOK DRIVE

INVERLEITH

INVERWOOD GDNS

ROCKVILLE CT

28

Slipway

Slipway

Victoria Park

Boating Lake

Playing Fields

Bowling Green

CONNSBANK RD

SYDENHAM BY-PASS

LARKFIELD DRIVE

LARKFIELD GDNS

Larkfield Manor

CONNSBROOK AVENUE

VICTORIA DRIVE

VICTORIA ROAD

VIDOR GDNS

LARKFIELD ROAD

Larkfield Ct

PALMERSTON ROAD

STATION ROAD

FB

Sydenham Station

Palmerston Pk

SYDENHAM

Youth Centre

VICTORIA ROAD

DEMISTOUN PARK

HOLYWOOD ROAD

CAROLHILL DRIVE

CAROLHILL GDNS

CAROLHILL PARK

Park

Playing Fields

Ashmore Park Mews

HELEN PK

Sydenham Pr Sch

STRANDBURN PARK

CONNSBROOK AVENUE

KERNIVAL STREET

PALMERSTON PDE

CLONAVER PARK

CLONAVER CRES NTH

CLONAVER DRIVE

CLONAVER CRES 6TH

CLONAVER COURT

NORWOOD CRES

NORWOOD PARK

Victoria Pk Hall

LANDSBROOK PARK

KYLE STREET

HILLS AVE

LISAVON DRIVE

LISAVON ST

PARK AVE

Strand Pr Sch

Connsbrook Drive

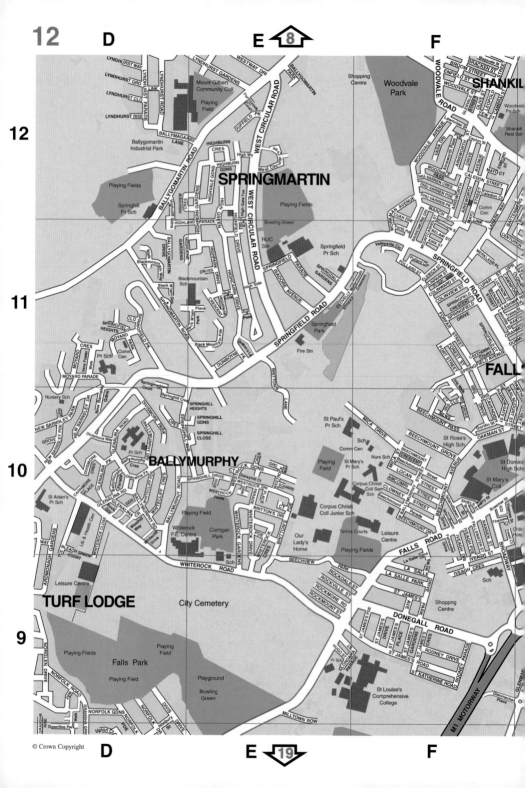

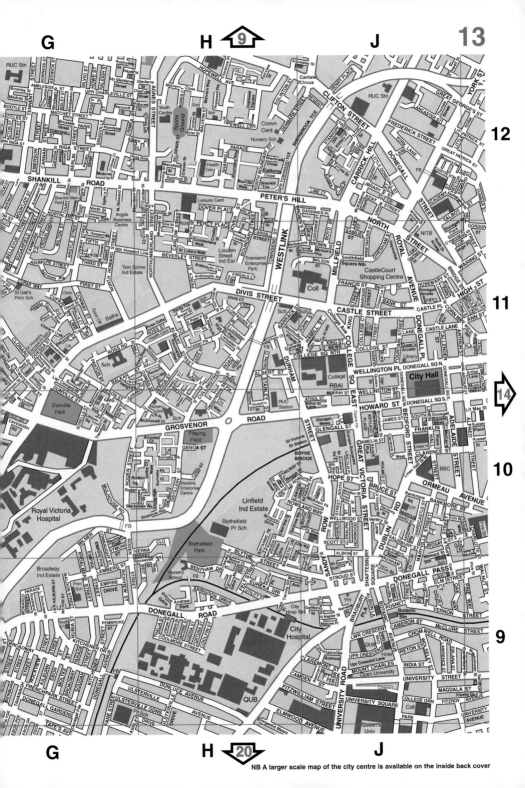

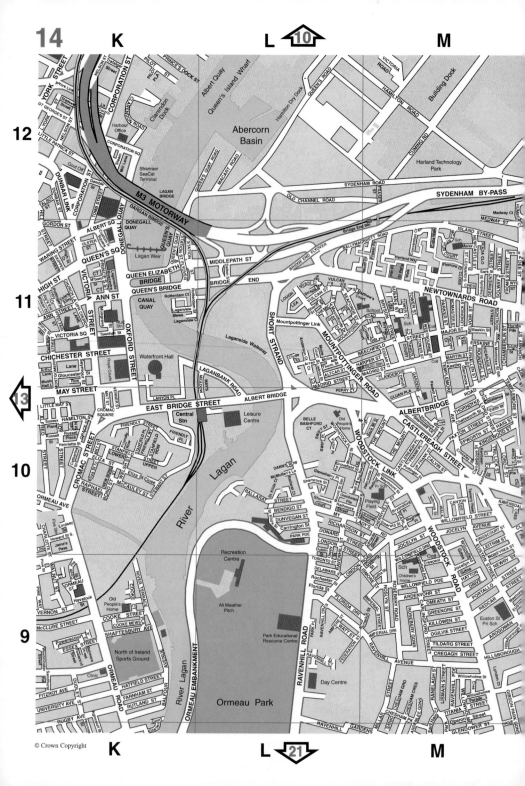

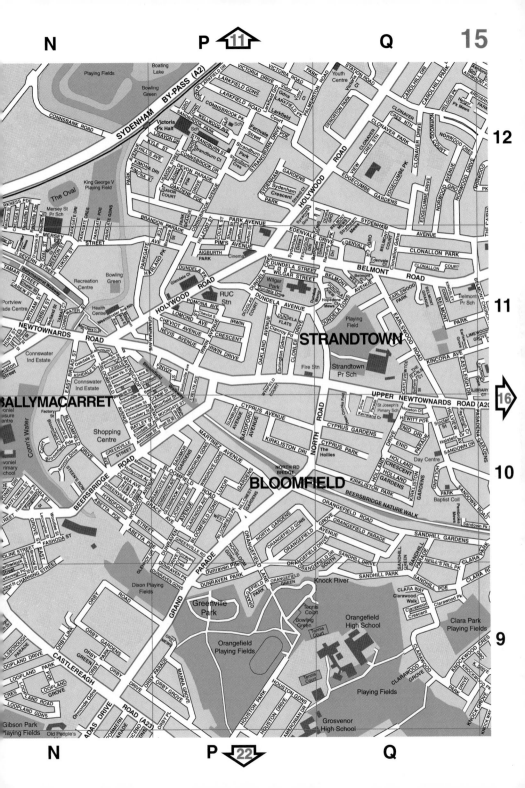

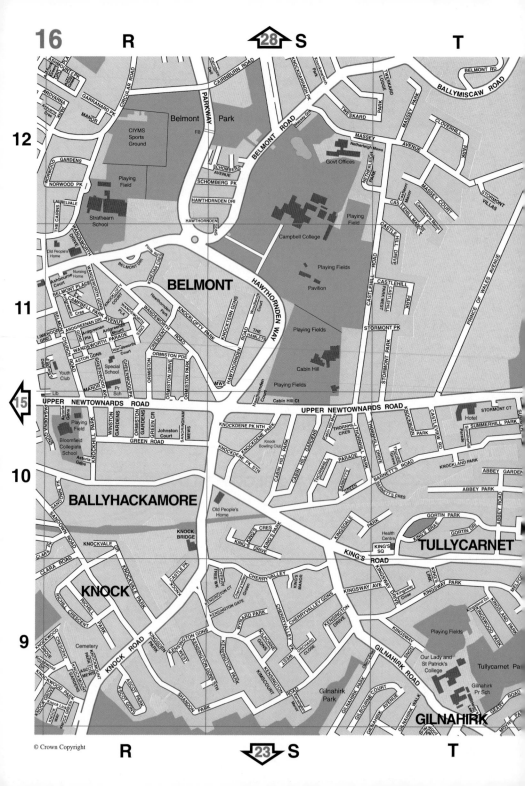

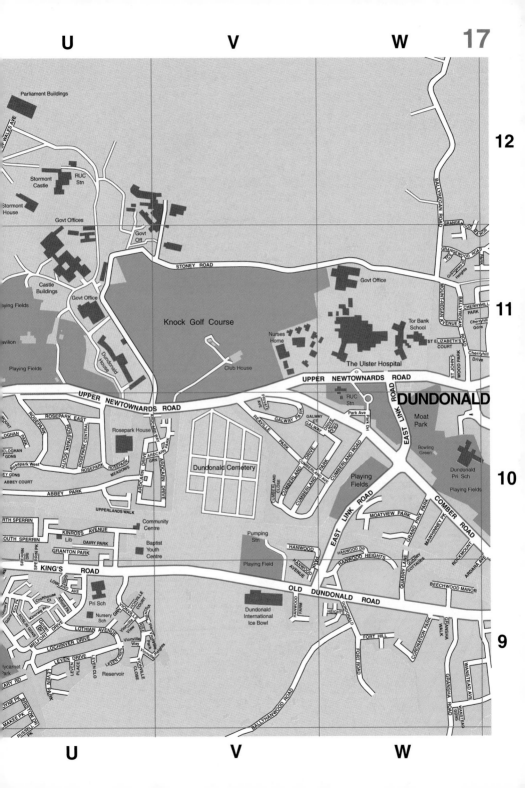

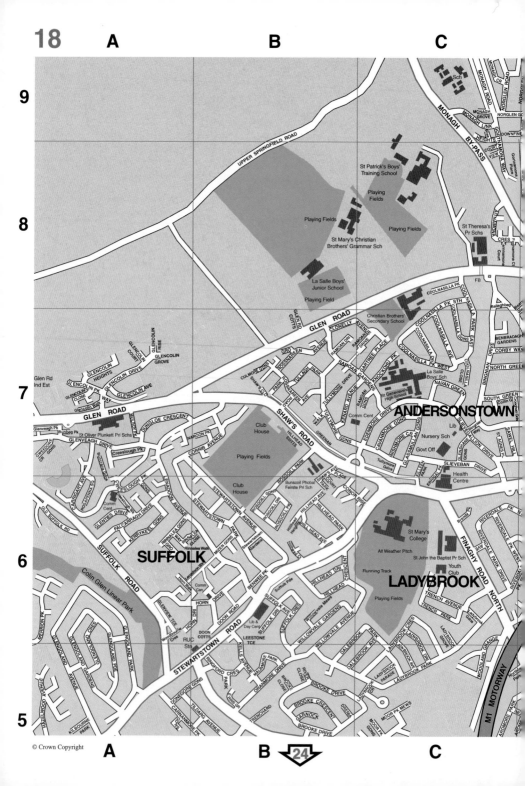

A   B   C

9

8

7

6

5

UPPER SPRINGFIELD ROAD

St Patrick's Boys' Training School

Playing Fields

Playing Fields

St Theresa's Pr Schs

Playing Fields

St Mary's Christian Brothers' Grammar Sch

La Salle Boys' Junior School

Playing Field

MONAGH BY-PASS

Sch

MONAGH ROAD

MONAGH GROVE

MONAGH LINK

MONAGH HEIGHTS

NORGLEN ROAD

NORGLEN CRES

NORGLEN GDNS

DOWNFINE

COURT

VIEW

Gartnamona Ct

RATHMORE

FB

Ballaghbeg

COOLNASILLA PK

COOLNASILLA PK STH

COOLNASILLA PK EAST

COOLNASILLA GDNS

COOLNASILLA PK WEST

COOLNASILLA

BENBRADAGH GARDENS

CORBY WAY

NORTH GREEN

BINGNIAN DRIVE

SOUTH GREEN

GLEN ROAD

GLEN ROAD

GLEN COTTS

GLEN RD

CLONELLY

CARTREE AVENUE

RANDALSTOWN

GARTREE PLACE

RAMOAN DRIVE

KNOCKDHU PK

La Salle Boys' Sch

St Genevieve's High School

NAVAN GREEN

Christian Brothers' Secondary School

GLENCOLIN RISE

GLENCOLIN COURT

GLENCOLIN GROVE

GLENCOLIN HEIGHTS

GLENCOLIN DRIVE

GLENCOLIN AVE

GLENCOLIN PK

GLENCOLIN CLOSE

GLENCOLIN WAY

Glencolin Walk

Glen Rd Ind Est

GLEN ROAD

Glenveagh Pk

Dunbeg Pk

St Oliver Plunkett Pri Schs

DINGLOE CRESCENT

HARROON PK

GLENVEAGH DRIVE

Creeslough Pk

CORRIB AVENUE

CULMORE GDNS

ROSSNAREEN

SHAW'S CLOSE

TULLAGH PARK

ROSSNAREEN AVE

PARK

TULLYMORE PARK

SHAW'S RD

SHAW'S ROAD

Club House

Playing Fields

Club House

ROSSCOILL PARK

Bunscoil Phobal Feirste Pri Sch

ROSSCOIL PARK

HILLHEAD AVE

HILLHEAD PARK

HILLHEAD DRI

HILLHEAD

SHAW'S PLACE

COSTA

COLINSON

RAMOAN DR

RAMOAN GDNS

EDENMORE DRIVE

GREENAN

Comm Cent

EDENMORE GDNS

CAVANMORE GDNS

WESTROCK GDNS

GLASSMULLAN GDNS

Tullymore Gdns

Tullymore Gdns

ANDERSONSTOWN

Lib

Nursery Sch

Govt Off

Health Centre

SLIEVEBAN DRIVE

SLIEVEBAN DRIVE

Collin Cl

GLENVEAGH DRIVE

SUFFOLK

SUFFOLK ROAD

Colin Glen Linear Park

OLD SUFFOLK RD

CARRIGART AVE

CREESLOUGH

GLENTIES DRIVE

Comm Cent

FALCARRAGH DRIVE

KIRKYKEEL

RINNALA GDNS

LENADOON AVENUE

STEWARTSTOWN ROAD

STEWARTSTOWN AVENUE

Rinnalea Walk

Lenadoon Wk

Stewartstown Gardens

BENNVEE PK

HORN DRIVE

HORN

HORN

WILLOWVALE GARDENS

WILLOWVALE AVENUE

Suffolk Pde

SUFFOLK DRI

SUFFOLK AVE

SUFFOLK CRES

Wigwam Men's

Lib & Day Cent

LEESTONE TCE

DOON COTTS

RUC Stn

KEALS AVENUE

BINGFORD CRES

ORANMORE DRIVE

CRANMORE PK

TILDARG AVENUE

CARNAMORE PK

BROOKE CRESCENT

BROOKE DRIVE

BROOKE DRIVE

GARNOCK

St Mary's College

All Weather Pitch

St John the Baptist Pr Sch

Running Track

LADYBROOK

Playing Fields

Youth Club

FINAGHY ROAD NORTH

RIVERDALE PK

RIVERDALE PARK DRIVE

RIVERDALE PK WEST

TRENCH AVENUE

TRENCH PARK

DALEBROOK AVE

DALEBROOK PARK

LADYBROOK PARADE

LADYBROOK AVENUE

LADYBROOK PARK

MOOR PK MEN'S

M1 MOTORWAY

RUTH WOOD AVENUE

KILBOURNE PARK

KILLEEN PARK

KERRON ST

A   B   C

24

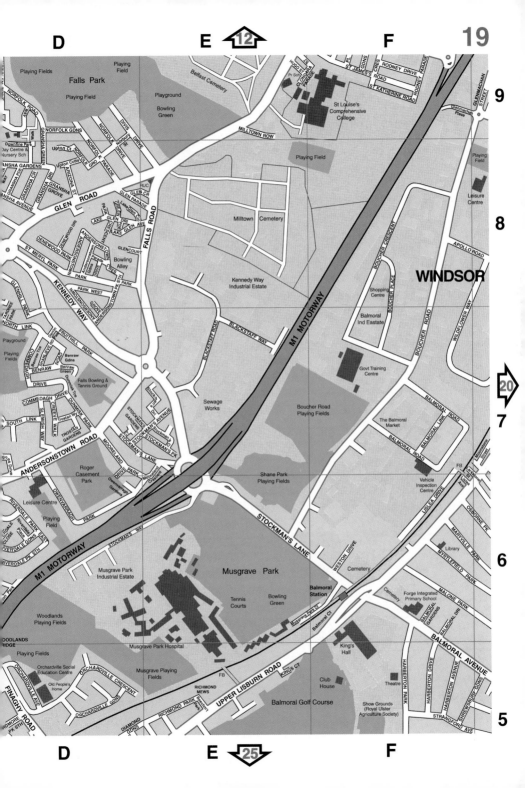

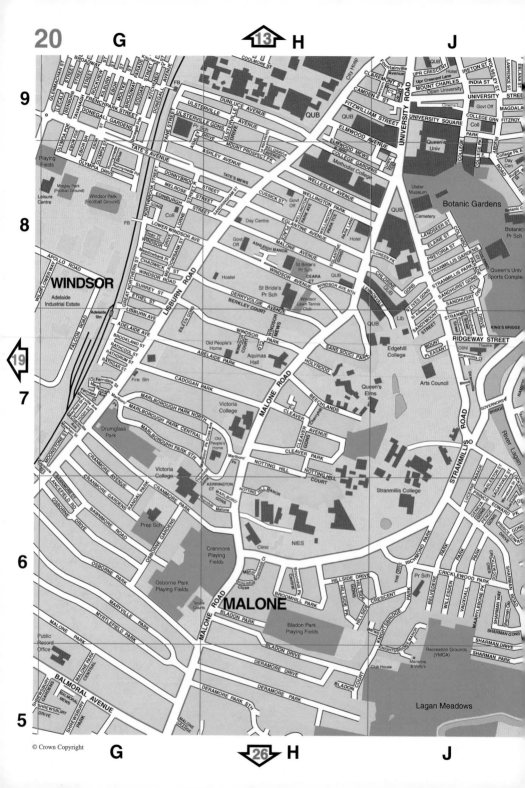

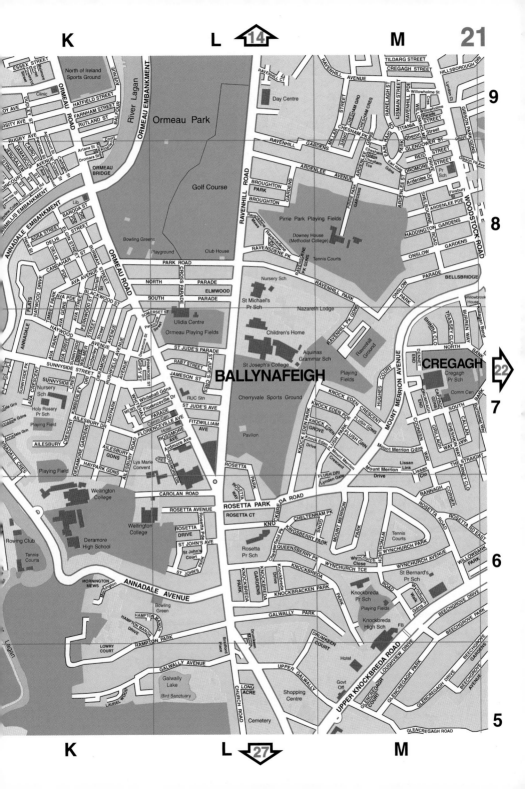

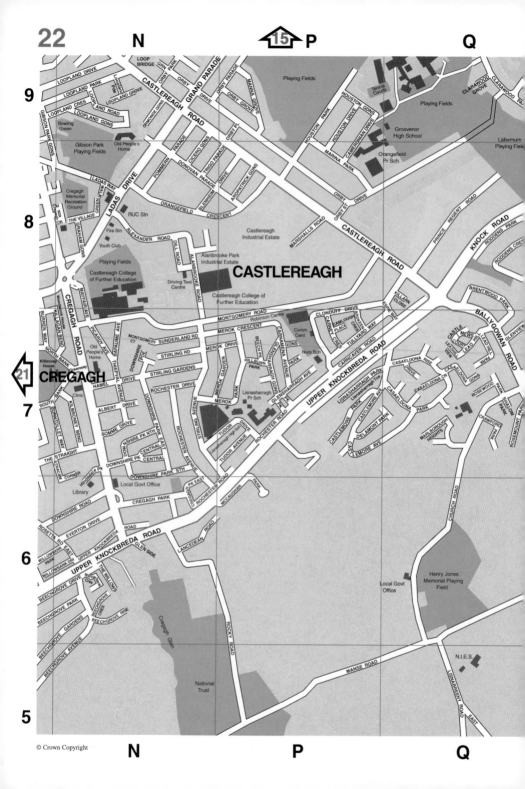

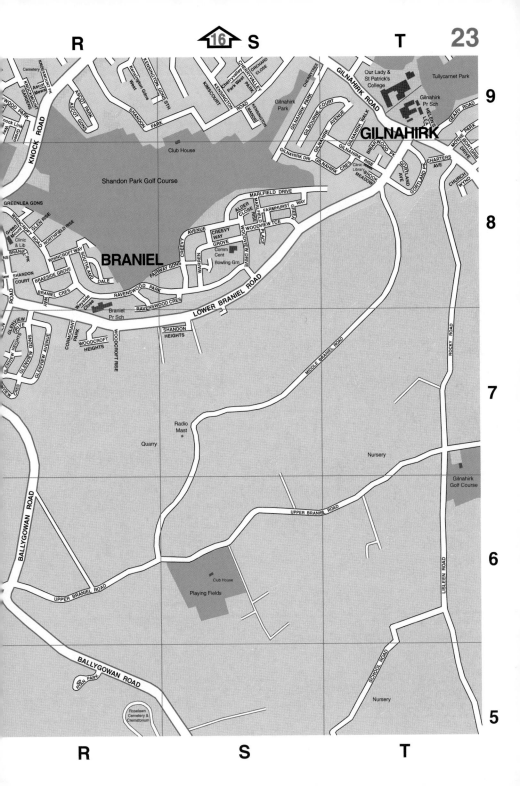

9

8

7

6

5

GILNAHIRK

BRANIEL

Our Lady & St Patrick's College

Tullycarnet Park

Gilnahirk Pr Sch

Gilnahirk Park

GILNAHIRK ROAD

GEARY ROAD

MONTGOMERY PK

Cemetery

KNOCKMOUNT PK

Ascot Mews

KNOCKMOUNT PK

WOOD PARK

Knock Link

KNOCK ROAD

ASCOT GDNS

ASCOT PARK

Kensington Gdns West

SHANDON PARK

KENSINGTON GDNS STH

KENSINGTON GARDENS

KENSINGTON ROAD

KIMSCOURT

KENSINGTON PARK

KENSINGTON MANOR

Sherry Valley Park West

ORCHARD CLOSE

CHERRY VALLEY

CHERRYTREE

GILNAHIRK PARK

GILBOURNE COURT

GILNAHIRK COURT

BRIARWOOD PK

GILNAHIRK WALK

GILNAHIRK AVENUE

GILNAHIRK RISE

HELEN'S LEA

GEARY ROAD

PARK DRIVE

Club House

Shandon Park Golf Course

Gilnahirk Park

GILNAHIRK DRI

GILNAHIRK

GILNAHIRK CRES

Clinic Library

BROOK MEADOW

SCOTLAND AVE

CHARTERS AVE

CHURCH WYND

GORTLAND PK

GREENLEA GDNS

Green MOUNT PK

GLEN RISE

WHINCROFT ROAD

NORTHFIELD RISE

Clinic & Lib

BRANIEL PK

WHINCROFT WAY

SCOTLAND

AVENUE

CREEVY WAY

FAIRWAY GDNS

WARREN

MARLFIELD DRIVE

ALDER CLOSE

MARLFIELD RISE

FARMHURST WAY

CREEVY WAY

WOODVIEW TCE

WOODVIEW PLACE

WOODVIEW DRIVE

CREEVY WAY GROVE

Comm Cent

Bowling Grn

MARLFIELD DRIVE

View SHANDON COURT

BRAESIDE GROVE

BRANIEL CRES

DALE

Wayside Close

RAVENSWOOD PARK

RAVENSWOOD CRES

LOWER BRANIEL ROAD

Braniel Pr Sch

GLENVIEW DRIVE

GLENVIEW HEIGHTS

GLENVIEW GDNS

GLENVIEW AVENUE

GLENVIEW CRES

GLENVIEW

CORMORANT PARK

WOODCROFT HEIGHTS

WOODCROFT RISE

SHANDON HEIGHTS

MIDDLE BRANIEL ROAD

ROCKY ROAD

Radio Mast

Quarry

Nursery

Gilnahirk Golf Course

BALLYGOWAN ROAD

UPPER BRANIEL ROAD

UPPER BRANIEL ROAD

Club House

Playing Fields

LISLEEN ROAD

BALLYGOWAN ROAD

Vista Park

SCHOOL ROAD

Nursery

Roselawn Cemetery & Crematorium

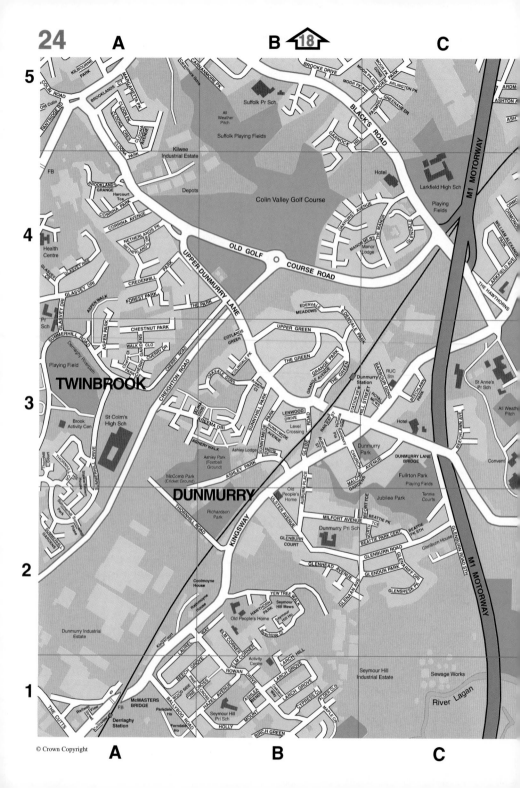

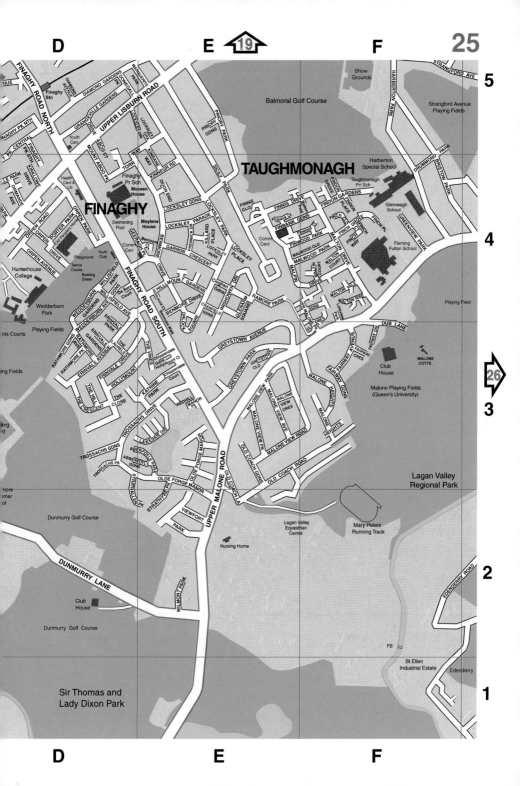

5

4

3

26

2

1

Show Grounds

Balmoral Golf Course

STRANGFORD AVE

Strangford Avenue Playing Fields

HARBERTON PARK

TAUGHMONAGH

Harberton Special School

Taughmonagh Pri Sch

Glenveagh School

Fleming Fulton School

DRUMMOND PARK

BRISTOW PARK

GREENVIEW PARK

FINAGHY ROAD NORTH

Finaghy Stn

DIAMOND GARDENS

GRANEVILLE GARDENS

UPPER LISBURN ROAD

PRIORY GDNS

STCELL PARK

Youth Cen

Finaghy Pr Sch
Moveen House

FINAGHY

Health Cent & Lib

MOUNT ABBOT RD

Swimming Pool

Moylena House

LOCKSLEY GDNS

LOCKSLEY PARK

LOCKSLEY PLACE

LOCKSLEY PLACE

FINNIS CLO

FINNIS DRIVE

FINBANK GDNS

Finbank

Comm Cent

FINWOOD PARK

MALWOOD CLO

MALWOOD PARK

FINCH GARDENS

FINOON GARDENS

FINCH PL

FINCH GROVE

FINCH WAY

MALTON DRIVE

MALTON COURT

Playground

Tennis Courts

Youth Club

Bowling Green

Comm Cent

BENMORE DRIVE

GARRON CRESCENT

KILLARD PLACE

Lockley Park

HILLMOUN GARDENS

RAMORE PARK

MALTON AVE

MALTON RISE

Hunterhouse College

Wedderburn Park

Playing Fields

ORPEN ROAD

ORPEN PARK

ORPEN AVENUE

ORPEN DRIVE

PORTERE PARK

FINAGHY ROAD SOUTH

WEDDERBURN GARDENS

WEDDERBURN AVE

WILLSFIELD AVE

ERINVALE PARK

ERINVALE GDNS

ERINVALE AVENUE

RATHMORE GDNS

RATHMORE PK

HOLLYMOUNT

THE VINES

THE HILL

THE CRESCENT

THE CLOSE

KATRINE PARK

REDHILL MANOR

GREYSTOWN AVENUE

GREYSTOWN CLO

GREYSTOWN PARK

MALONE VIEW PARK

MALONE VIEW CRES

MALONE VIEW AVE

MALONE HEIGHTS

FAIRWAY AVENUE

FAIRWAY GDNS

FAIRWAY CRES

DUB LANE

Club House

MALONE COTTS

Playing Field

Malone Playing Fields (Queen's University)

Lagan Valley Regional Park

TROSSACHS GDNS

TROSSACHS PK

ABERFOYLE MANOR

ABERFOYLE GDNS

STRATHALLEN

OLDE FORGE MANOR

UPPER MALONE ROAD

OLD COACH ROAD

OLD COACH ROAD

VIEWFORT PARK

Dunmurry Golf Course

WILMONT PARK

Nursing Home

Lagan Valley Equestrian Centre

Mary Peters Running Track

DUNMURRY LANE

Club House

Dunmurry Golf Course

EDENDERRY ROAD

FB

St Ellen Industrial Estate

Edenderry

Sir Thomas and Lady Dixon Park

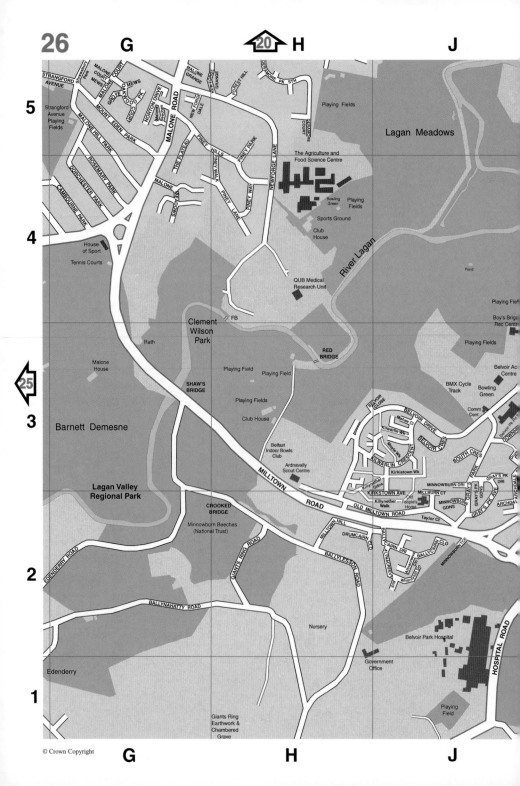

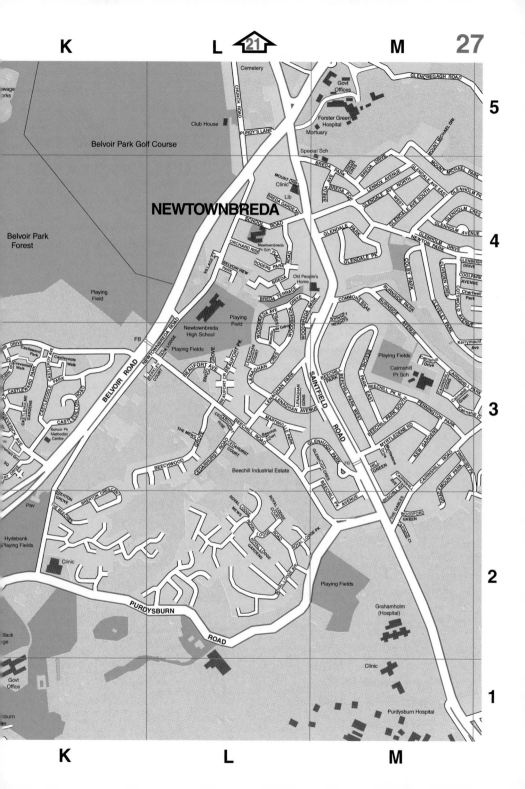

5

Cemetery

GLENCREGAGH ROAD

Govt Offices

Forster Green Hospital

Mortuary

Club House

PURDY'S LANE

CHURCH ROAD

Belvoir Park Golf Course

Special Sch

MOUNT MICHAEL DRI

MOUNT MICHAEL PARK

BREDA DRIVE

BREDA PARK

BREDA AVE

LENNOX AVENUE

GLENDALE AVE NORTH

GLENDALE AVE EAST

GLENHOLM PK

GLENDALE AVE WEST

GLENDALE AVE SOUTH

GLENHOLM CRES

GLENHOLM AVENUE

GLENHOLM DRIVE

MOUNT OBIEL Clinic

BREDA RD

Lib

BREDA GARDENS

4

NEWTOWNBREDA

Belvoir Park Forest

SCHOOL ROAD

ORCHARD RISE

Newtownbreda Pr Sch

ROGERS PARK

VILLAGE ST

BELVOIR VIEW PARK

GLENDALE PARK

GLENDALE PK

NEWTON PARK

COLBY PARK

GLENBEIGH DRIVE

COOLPARK

Playing Field

Old People's Home

BREDA

BREDA TERRACE

CLIVEDEN CRES

CHARTWELL Park

COTSWOLD AVENUE

Playing Field

Newtownbreda High School

WOODBREDA DRIVE

WOODBREDA AVE

Breda Gdns

COMMONS BRAE

BURNSIDE PARK

BURNSIDE AVENUE

WHINNEY HEIGHTS

FISK LODGE

FB

Playing Fields

Playing Fields

Cairnshill Drive

Cairnshill Pr Sch

BEAUFORT AVE

BEAUFORT CRES

BEAUFORT PK

SWOD

BEECHILL COURT

LENAGHAN AVE

LENAGHAN CRES

LENAGHAN PARK

LENAGHAN GDNS

LENAGHAN AVENUE

BEECHILL ROAD

SAINTFIELD ROAD

BEECHILL PARK WEST

BEECHILL PARK EAST

BEECHILL PK N

PENNINGTON PARK

CAIRNSHILL PARK

Cairnshill Green

KERRYMOUNT Ave

CASTLEWARD PARK

Crevenish Walk

CASTLECOOLE Walk

CASTLECOOLE PARK

CASTLE WELLAN ROAD

CASTLEHUME GARDENS

CASTLE ... LIME

ROAD DRIVE

Belvoir Pk Methodist Centre

THE MEWS

CEDARHURST ROAD

CEDARHURST RISE

CEDARHURST COURT

MARTINVALE PARK

Beechill Court

GLENHUGH PARK

GLENHUGH CRES

BEECHILL PARK SOUTH

MYRTLE DENE RD

KEW GARDENS

CAIRNSHILL ROAD

FIREFLY PK

3

BEECHWOOD

Beechill Industrial Estate

BEECHILL PK AVENUE

FB

HILL GREEN

MEECHILL AVE MEWS

MYrtle Mews

THE GABLES

GRAHAMMOUNT PARK

Pav

ROBERTON GROVE

BREEEN CRESCENT

THE BEECHES

ROYAL LODGE MEWS

ROYAL LODGE COURT

ROYAL LODGE ROAD

ROYAL LODGE PK

ROYAL LODGE GARDENS

WOODFORD GREEN

SYBIL Ct

2

Hydebank Playing Fields

Clinic

Playing Fields

Grahamholm (Hospital)

Black ... ge

PURDYSBURN ROAD

ROAD

Clinic

1

Govt Office

...sburn

Purdysburn Hospital

sewage ...orks

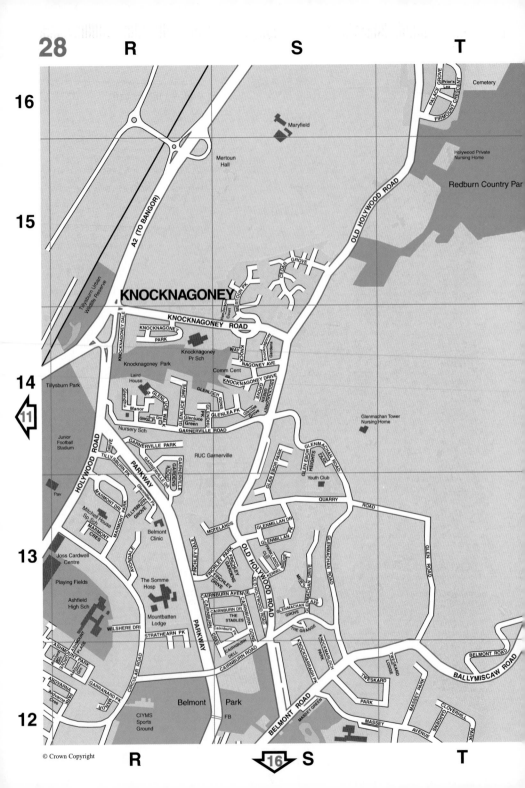

Due to insufficient space, some streets and/or their names have been omitted from the street map. Street names below which are prefixed by a * are not represented on the map, but they can be located by referring in the index to the name of the street which follows in brackets.

STREET INDEX

STREET INDEX

31

STREET INDEX

STREET INDEX

STREET INDEX

38

STREET INDEX

STREET INDEX

Belfast, like so many other cities, grew up on the banks of a river - its Irish name, Béal Feirste, means 'the mouth of the sandy ford'. It enjoys a beautiful setting on the shores of Belfast Lough, sheltered on one side by the mountains of Antrim and on the other by the green hills of County Down. The city itself fails to live up the beauty of its setting, lacking the graciousness of Dublin, a reflection of the fact that Belfast's city fathers were Victorian industrialists rather than Anglo Irish aristocrats. Thirty years of 'Troubles' have left their mark but the tide has turned in recent years, and Belfast is definitely on the up and up, with billions of pounds of investment helping to regenerate the city, most notably along the banks of the River Lagan.

Belfast's native population was largely undisturbed by visitors until the Anglo Normans arrived in the 12th century. Its defences were strengthened with a castle built by the knight adventurer John de Courcy in 1177 but Norman power was eroded by an onslaught from the Gaelic clans, most notably the O'Neills of Clandeboye.

By 1542, Henry VIII had proclaimed himself King of Ireland as well as England, and the Reformation came to Ireland. In 1603 Sir Arthur Chichester was sent by James I to mastermind the Plantation of Ulster, which saw the arrival of thousands of Lowland Scots and the beginning of the Protestant Ascendancy. By 1613, King James had granted Belfast a charter of incorporation, which can still be seen today in the City Hall, and the town had taken its first step on the road to becoming a major city.

With Charles I beheaded and the English monarchy abolished, Oliver Cromwell landed in Ireland with a large army in 1649, ushering in a particularly bloody and savage era in Irish history. By the time the monarchy was restored in 1660, Belfast was a prosperous port, shipping produce from Plantation farms to Britain and abroad. English and Scottish settlers continued to flood in and the town's population was overwhelmingly Protestant at a time when Catholics made up most of the population of Ireland.

By 1685 the Catholic King James II was on the throne and Ireland was set to become a battlefield for a religious war involving most of Europe's major powers. In 1690 King James lost the Battle of the Boyne to the Protestant William of Orange who went on to become king. This victory is still commemorated today by thousands of Ulster Orangemen with parades throughout Northern Ireland every year on the 12th of July. After defeat at the Battle of the Boyne Catholics and other non-Anglicans suffered under the Penal Laws, Gaelic culture was driven underground, and the seeds were sewn for the struggle for Irish autonomy from England. Implementation of the Penal Laws by the English

forged an unlikely alliance between Belfast's middle class Presbyterians and Catholics, who together sought basic rights for all and a transfer of power from the English ruling class. Inspired by the American War of Independence and stirrings of revolution in France, a group of merchants led by Henry Joy McCracken and the Dublin revolutionary, Wolfe Tone, founded the Society of United Irishmen in 1791. Their efforts to unite the people of Ireland against English Rule foundered with the failed 1798 Rebellion. Rebel leaders were hanged, the Irish Parliament in Dublin was abolished, and the Act of Union of 1800 brought Ireland into a United Kingdom with Britain, with the seat of political power in Ireland moving from Dublin to Westminster.

A century of political turmoil followed. Daniel O'Connell helped to achieve Catholic emancipation in 1829 and, as Protestant influence weakened, sectarian tensions rose in Belfast and sporadic violence ensued. Economically, however, things were looking up. The Industrial Revolution saw Belfast grow from a small town into one of the world's major commercial ports. Belfast thrived on the development of its ship building and textile industries and, when Queen Victoria visited in 1888, she granted city status at a time when the population had grown to more than 300,000.

Political storm clouds continued to gather, however. The famine years of the 1840's had heightened anti British sentiment in Ireland, and an abortive rebellion by the Irish Republican Brotherhood in 1868 led to calls for Irish Home Rule. The case for Irish autonomy was taken up in the English parliament at Westminster by the Protestant leader Charles Stewart Parnell. Parnell died in 1891 and the political vacuum which resulted was eventually filled by a new breed of political nationalism with the establishment of Sinn Fein (Ourselves Alone), a political movement which advocated a boycott of the English Parliament.

As momentum towards Home Rule increased, Unionists in Ulster rallied to oppose it and made clear their willingness to use force if necessary. Belfast had prospered as part of the British Empire and Unionists feared Catholic domination and economic decline in the event of an independent Ireland.

With Britain engaged in the First World War, Sinn Fein organised the occupation of several strategic buildings around Dublin and declared an Irish republic from its headquarters in the General Post Office on Easter Monday 1916.

The Easter Rising was quashed after six days of fighting with British forces, who numbered 20,000 troops, and 15 of the rebel leaders were later executed. A wave of public sympathy resulted and Sinn Fein secured an overwhelming victory in the 1918 elections.

Growing divergence between the mainly Catholic

Belfast's new Waterfront Hall and Hilton Hotel

The advent of the Welfare State led to improvements in the quality of life for Belfast's citizens after the Second World War, but the concentration of power in the hands of Unionists led to dissatisfaction among many Catholic nationalists who felt that they were being discriminated against when it came to jobs, housing and political power.

When the Civil Rights Association marched in Derry in 1968 demanding 'one man, one vote' in council elections, there were violent scenes. By August 1969 sectarian violence was flaring in Belfast and the British army was sent in to separate Catholic and Protestant communities. By 1972, the British government had disbanded the Northern Ireland Parliament at Stormont and power was transferred back to London. By this time the IRA had been reactivated and a nationalist campaign was under way to achieve British withdrawal from Northern Ireland.

Press and television conveyed pictures of Belfast as a war zone for the next twenty five years. Since the first paramilitary ceasefires of 1994, however, the city has experienced a seachange in both atmosphere and environment. Physical barriers for the most part have been removed while work continues to bridge religious and political divisions. Times have definitely changed for the better though, and visitors are invariably impressed with the air of normality around Belfast these days.

Cultural life never disappeared, even during the worst years of the Troubles, but as people dedicate more of their energies to everyday leisure activities, the arts are raising their profile in the city. Leading lights include the Ulster Orchestra and its spectacular new home, Belfast's Waterfront Hall, the critically acclaimed Opera Northern Ireland who perform amid the Victorian splendour of the Grand Opera House, the Lyric Theatre who nurtured the talents of Liam Neeson when he was still speaking with a Ballymena accent, and the Belfast Festival at Queen's which takes place every year in November.

When it boils down to it, however, its people are Belfast's greatest asset, even if they also represent its greatest liability! Like the harshness of the local accent, there is a bluntness associated with the local character - they like to call a spade a spade - but there is also a warmth, friendliness and, above all, good humour, although it pays to recognise irony at fifty paces as many of the best lines heard in Belfast are delivered with a straight face.

Whether it's novelty value, or simply a natural interest in people, especially people from farther afield, Belfast is particularly welcoming to tourists and visitors to the city. Whether you are living here or just passing through, the sections which follow try to point you in the right direction and aim to ensure that you make the best of all that Belfast has to offer.

Nationalists and the mainly Protestant Unionists was highlighted by the fact that 5,500 men from the Ulster Division died for Britain during the Battle of the Somme, only months after the Easter Rising in Dublin. This helped to strengthen the already strong bonds between Britain and Unionists in the north of Ireland, and it was clear by that time that Ulster could not be forced into an independent Ireland.

A War of Independence between British and Irish republican armies soon followed the 1918 elections and, after two years of fighting, the IRA general, Michael Collins, signed a treaty in 1921 which resulted in the creation of the Irish Free State, comprising 26 of Ireland's 32 counties. The other six counties became known as Northern Ireland and remained within the United Kingdom, although government powers were transferred from London to a new, Unionist-dominated parliament, based at Stormont on the outskirts of Belfast. Collins said at the time that he was signing his own death warrant and he was proved right the following year.

The birth of Northern Ireland came at an inauspicious time. The Great Depression of the 1920's crippled the industries upon which Belfast had been built. The Second World War brought some respite with a sharp increase in ship and aircraft production although the city suffered heavy bombing during the Blitz of 1941.

AIR TRAVEL

Belfast has two airports, Belfast International and Belfast City. Scheduled flights are shared pretty evenly between the two with the vast majority of scheduled traffic destined for British airports. With a few exceptions, most international flights are chartered and tend to depart from Belfast International.

Belfast International Airport

Known locally as Aldergrove, Belfast International is located about 18 miles north-west of the city centre and is served by a good road network which links it to all parts of Northern Ireland. Passenger facilities, which include hotel accommodation, put Belfast International among the best regional airports in Europe and allow it to cope comfortably with the 2.5 million passengers who use it annually.

The terminal building contains a good selection of shops, bars and restaurants, and special facilities for the disabled. The arrivals concourse contains several car hire desks, bureau de change facilities and an information desk which provides tourist information and a booking service for accommodation anywhere in Ireland. A 10% deposit and a booking fee of up to £2 are payable at the time of booking.

An express bus service to Belfast leaves every half hour (every hour in the evening) from in front of the terminal building. Buses stop in the city centre at Laganside Buscentre and at the Europa Buscentre, which is adjacent to Great Victoria Street railway station, and the journey time is around half an hour. Tickets currently cost £4.50 for a single journey. For details of onward journeys by bus or train to other parts of Northern Ireland and to the Republic of Ireland see pages 46-50.

The airport's taxi rank is also in front of the terminal building and the journey to the centre of Belfast takes about twenty minutes and costs about £20. If you prefer to hire a car, Avis, Europcar, Hertz and McCausland all have reception desks in the arrivals concourse.

As far as car parking is concerned, there is a choice of Short Stay, Main Stay, and Holiday Car Parks. Prices start at around £1 for half an hour in the Short Stay, and alternative tariffs include one week in the Holiday Car Park for around £10. Off-airport parking is available outside the airport entrance and a courtesy coach service is provided to convey passengers to the terminal building.

For further information and details on all flights from Belfast International Airport, telephone 01849 422888.

Belfast City Airport

The City Airport is situated on the main Belfast to Bangor Road, the A2, less than 10 minutes drive from the city centre. The airport offers ready access to a much improved road network linking Belfast with the rest of Northern Ireland, and bus and rail links are less than 5 minutes walk from the terminal building.

The terminal building has benefited from an ongoing programme of investment since scheduled services first took off in 1983, and facilities have been upgraded to cope with passenger figures which now exceed one million per year.

An information desk is situated inside the terminal entrance which provides tourist information and a booking service for accommodation anywhere in Ireland. A 10% deposit and a booking fee of up to £2 are payable at the time of booking. The departure area includes a public bar, restaurant, gift shop, Nursing Mother & Baby Room, and a cash dispenser. Car hire can be arranged in the arrivals area.

There is a taxi rank in front of the terminal building and the journey into the city centre is quick and inexpensive. Alternatively, Sydenham railway station is only five minutes walk from the terminal building. Access is by the footbridge at the airport entrance and the journey time to Belfast Central Station is about five minutes (see Trains on pages 46 & 47). A frequent Citybus service operates into the city centre from Station Road, which is just beyond the train station. The service number is 21 and the journey time is about 20 minutes (see Buses on pages 48-50). If you prefer to hire a car, Avis, Europcar, Hertz Budget and McCausland all have desks in the arrivals within the terminal building.

Car parks are situated close to the the airport entrance and a courtesy bus is provided to take you the short distance to the terminal building. The Long Stay Car Park costs around £2 per day and prices for the Short Stay Car Park start at around £1 for the first hour.

For flight and other airport information telephone 457745

FERRY SERVICES

The number of routes connecting Northern Ireland to Great Britain has increased significantly in recent years.

Stena Line operate services between Belfast and Stanraer which is on the West coast of Scotland. The passenger terminal is on Corry Road and bookings can be made by phoning 747747.

P&O European Ferries operate services between Larne, which is about 25 miles north of Belfast, and

Cairnryan, which is only a few miles from Stranraer. P&O operate another service from Larne which crosses to Fleetwood on the north west coast of England. Reservations for both services can be made by phoning 0870 2424777.

Norse Irish Ferries cross from Belfast to Liverpool and reservations can be made by phoning 779090.

Sea Containers Ferries operate services from Belfast to Stranraer, from Belfast to the Isle of Man, and from Ballycastle on the Antrim coast to Campelltown in the north west of Scotland. Reservations can be made on 0990 523523.

TRAINS

The public transport system in Northern Ireland is integrated into a single group called Translink which incorporates Northern Ireland Railways, Ulsterbus and Citybus.

Northern Ireland Railways operate rail services within Northern Ireland as well as providing links to the Republic of Ireland, Britain and Europe. Central Station on East Bridge Street (p14 K10) stands at the hub of the rail network (see route map opposite). The station is a ten minute walk from the city centre, but a shuttle bus service called Centrelink runs between Central Station, the Europa Buscentre, the Laganside Buscentre and the city centre. The service is free to most bus and rail passengers. Great Victoria Street Station is a more convenient stop if you want to shop in the centre of town, while Botanic Station is your best bet if you are looking for a night out on the town.

Dublin Trains

The train journey to Dublin has been transformed in recent years with investment in new rolling stock and a continuing programme of line improvements which have cut the journey time to around two hours with further time savings to come. The first train leaves Central Station at 6.45am, getting you into Dublin for 9am, and departures are roughly every couple of hours thereafter, until the last train leaves just after 8pm.

Saver Tickets

There is a wide range of special saver tickets available which allow unlimited rail travel over a set number of days. These tickets can be bought at Central Station and should be purchased before you travel:

Freedom of Northern Ireland: valid for one, three or seven days of unlimited travel on all scheduled bus and rail services in Northern Ireland operated by Northern Ireland Railways, Citybus and Ulsterbus. Cost is cur-

rently £10 for one day, £25 for three days and £37 for seven days.

Irish Rover: valid for five days of rail travel throughout the whole of Ireland within a fifteen day period.

Emerald Card: valid for 8 days of unlimited travel on scheduled bus and rail services throughout Ireland within a 15 day period, or 15 days travel within a 30 day period.

Travelling by train is especially cheap on Sundays when £3 will currently buy unlimited rail travel within Northern Ireland. A family ticket allows travel by two adults and two children and currently costs £7.50.Tickets must be purchased and the outward journey made before 3pm.

For details of all rail services phone 899411.

BUS SERVICES

Along with NIR, the bus system in Belfast and Northern Ireland is integrated into a single group called Translink but, for practical purposes, you will find yourself boarding either a Citybus or an Ulsterbus. Citybus services tend to start or finish close to the City Hall, right in the heart of the city centre, and radiate out to all parts of the greater Belfast area. More information is provided below under the Citybus heading and a map of the city centre departure points can be found on page 48.

The Ulsterbus network, on the other hand, connects all the major towns and cities in Northern Ireland. Ulsterbus services extend to destinations in the Republic of Ireland, the UK mainland, and even on to mainland Europe. The network is operated under different service names and each is outlined below under the Ulsterbus heading. Both Ulsterbus and Citybus operate a no smoking policy.

Citybus

As mentioned above, the focal point for Citybus services is Belfast City Hall which is situated in Donegall Square. Buses leave from different points, all within the vicinity of the City Hall, and tickets and information for all routes are available from the Citybus Kiosk which is situated on Donegall Square West. See map of departure points on page 48.

Fares can be paid in cash to the driver when boarding a Citybus, but a range of multi-journey tickets and travel cards can be purchased from the Citybus Kiosk in Donegall Square West or from the large number of ticket agents located in newsagents, sweet shops and

Northern Ireland Railways Network Map

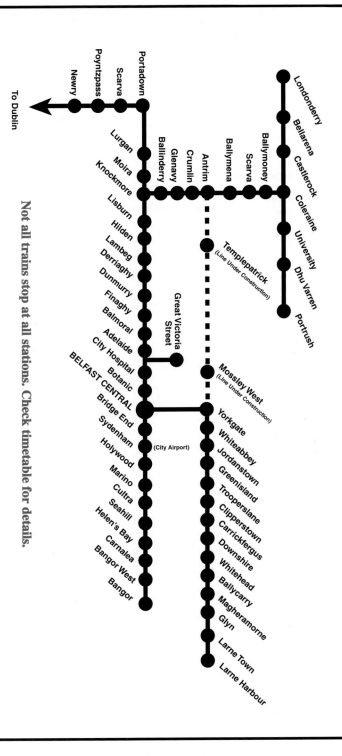

Not all trains stop at all stations. Check timetable for details.

To Dublin

Newry
Poyntzpass
Scarva
Portadown

Lurgan
Moira
Knockmore
Lisburn
Hilden
Lambeg
Derriaghy
Dunmurry
Finaghy
Balmoral
Adelaide
City Hospital
Botanic
BELFAST CENTRAL
Bridge End
Sydenham (City Airport)
Holywood
Marino
Cultra
Seahill
Helen's Bay
Carnalea
Bangor West
Bangor

Ballinderry
Glenavy
Crumlin
Antrim

Great Victoria Street

Ballymena
Scarva
Ballymoney

Templepatrick
(Line Under Construction)

Mossley West
(Line Under Construction)

Yorkgate
Whiteabbey
Jordanstown
Greenisland
Trooperslane
Clipperstown
Carrickfergus
Downshire
Whitehead
Ballycarry
Magheramorne
Glyn
Larne Town
Larne Harbour

Londonderry
Bellarena
Castlerock
Coleraine
University
Dhu Varren
Portrush

CityBus

City Centre Departure Points Monday to Saturday
(All Sunday services leave from Donegall Square West)

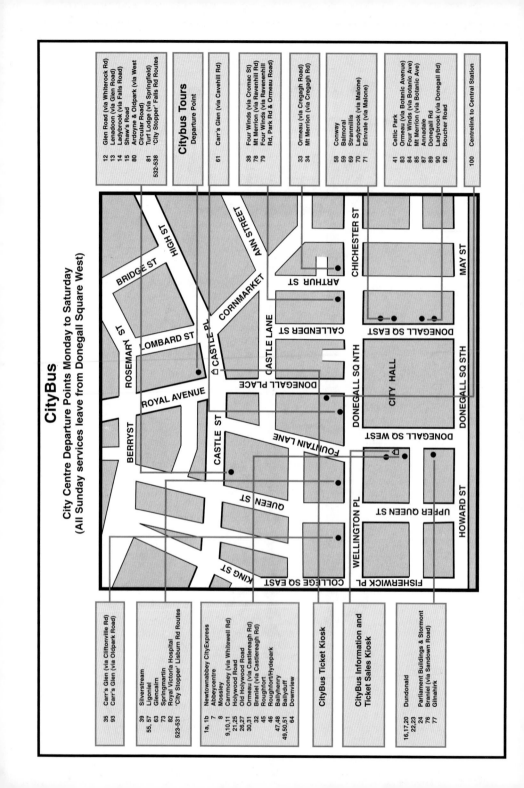

12	Glen Road (via Whiterock Rd)
13	Lenadoon (via Glen Road)
14	Ladybrook (via Falls Road)
15	Shaw's Road
80	Ardoyne & Oldpark (via West Circular Road)
81	Turf Lodge (via Springfield)
532-538	'City Stopper' Falls Rd Routes

Citybus Tours
Departure Point

61	Carr's Glen (via Cavehill Rd)

38	Four Winds (via Cromac St)
78	Mt Merrion (via Ravenhill Rd)
79	Four Winds (via Ravenenhill Rd, Park Rd & Ormeau Road)

33	Ormeau (via Cregagh Road)
34	Mt Merrion (via Cregagh Rd)

58	Conway
59	Balmoral
69	Stranmillis
70	Ladybrook (via Malone)
71	Erinvale (via Malone)

41	Celtic Park
83	Ormeau (via Botanic Avenue)
84	Four Winds (via Botanic Ave)
85	Mt Merrion (via Botanic Ave)
87	Annadale
89	Donegall Rd
90	Ladybrook (via Donegall Rd)
92	Boucher Road

100	Centrelink to Central Station

35	Carr's Glen (via Cliftonville Rd)
93	Carr's Glen (via Oldpark Road)

39	Silverstream
55, 57	Ligoniel
63	Glencairn
73	Springmartin
82	Royal Victoria Hospital
523-531	'City Stopper' Lisburn Rd Routes

1a, 1b	Newtownabbey CityExpress
7	Abbeycentre
8	Mossley
9,10,11	Carnmoney (via Whitewell Rd)
21,25	Holywood Road
26,27	Old Holywood Road
30,31	Ormeau (via Castlereagh Rd)
32	Braniel (via Castlereagh Rd)
45	Roughfort
46	Roughfort/Hydepark
47,48	Ballyhenry
49,50,51	Ballyduff
64	Downview

CityBus Ticket Kiosk

CityBus Information and Ticket Sales Kiosk

16,17,20	Dundonald
22,23	Parliament Buildings & Stormont
24	
76	Braniel (via Sandown Road)
77	Gilnahirk

post offices throughout the city. **For details of all Citybus services phone 246485.**

Citybus Tours

Citybus Tours operate mainly during the summer months from June to October but some tours operate throughout the year:

Belfast City Tour, which has been operating since 1985, lets you view and enjoy many of the varied features which Belfast has to offer. The tour departs from Castle Place Monday to Saturday at 1.30pm and lasts approximately three and a half hours. Cost is currently £8.50 which includes refreshments and a souvenir booklet.

Belfast : A Living History, which takes in many of Belfast's historical places, leaves every Thursday and Sunday at 1pm from Castle Place.The cost of this tour is also £8.50 which again includes refreshments and a souvenir booklet.

The Lagan Experience leaves from Castle Place at 1pm on Wednesday and lasts for around three and a half hours. The tour, which costs £10, includes entry to the Lagan Lookout (see page 55) and a river boat trip.

Other tours include a one hour tour of Belfast which allows you to hop on or off as you please (**Belfast City Wanderer**), a scenic tour of North Down, and a tour which looks at the production process of linen. Tour details are subject to frequent change and so it is best to check details beforehand. Advance booking is advisable and can be made at the Citybus Kiosk, Donegall Square West or credit card bookings can be made by phone on 458484.

Late Night Services

Citybus operates its Nightline service on five citywide routes, departing from Shaftesbury Square at midnight, 1am, and 2am every Friday and Saturday night. Tickets must be bought in advance from the ticket office in Shaftesbury Square between 9pm and 1.50 a.m. - they are not available from the drivers. For further information, telephone 246485.

Ulsterbus

As mentioned earlier, Ulsterbus operates a comprehensive network of services which connects all the major towns in Northern Ireland. Services extend to destinations in the Republic of Ireland, Great Britain, and even on to mainland Europe. Ulsterbus (blue buses) do not carry local passengers within Belfast city boundary except for services with a number in the 500 series which are known as City Stoppers, and on Sundays when all Ulsterbus services (except expresses) stop to pick up and set down in the Citybus area. As you may already have gathered, Ulsterbus services are operated under different service names and some more are outlined below.

Goldline Express Services

The Ulsterbus Goldline service links all the major towns within Northern Ireland, and includes the Maiden City Flyer which operates between Belfast and Londonderry (journey time 1 hour 40 minutes), and a Belfast to Dublin service with at least four departures every day (journey time approximately three hours).

Belfast services operate out of either Laganside Buscentre (p14 K11) or the Europa Buscentre in Glengall Street (p13 J10). Both stations are bright and modern, waiting is done in comfort, food and refreshments are on hand, and staff are on hand to handle any inquiries or booking requirements. The inter-city services tend to depart from the Europa Buscentre.

Airbus

An excellent airport shuttle service operates between Belfast International Airport and Belfast city centre. One or two coaches an hour leave from the Europa Buscentre between 5.45am and 9.30pm Monday to Saturday, with a slightly less frequent service operating between 6.30am and 8.45pm on Sundays. The return service leaves from in front of the main terminal building between 7.10am and 11.20pm Monday to Saturday. Sunday departures, once again, are slightly less frequent, operating between 6.50am and 11.20pm. A special timetable operates on Public Holidays. Fares at the time of writing are £4.50 single and £7.50 return and journey time is approximately 30 minutes. Wheelchair space on the Airbus may be booked in advance by telephoning (01232) 337008.

Flexibus

Flexibus operates a fleet of 19 & 25 seat mini-coaches for private hire, with drivers, for varied travel requirements in and outside Ireland. Wheelchair facilities are provided for the disabled. Flexibus also operate a number of late night services to and from Belfast on Fridays and Saturdays, and a shuttle service linking the Seacat Terminal with Belfast City Centre. Information on the Nightrider service and other Flexibus services is available from the Europa Buscentre or by telephoning 337003.

Ulsterbus DayTours

Ulsterbus DayTours operate mainly during the summer

months, but a programme of tours is also available for Easter and the May Public Holidays. Destinations are too numerous to mention but include most of the province's resorts and beauty spots. Variety even extends to a tour which visits Daniel O'Donnell at his home in Donegal during his annual open day. Daniel, with the help of his mammy, once managed to serve tea to 7,000 fans in a single day! All DayTours depart from the Europa Buscentre, Glengall Street. Bookings can be made in person at the Travel Centre in the Europa Buscentre. Enquiries can be made on 333000.

Ulsterbus Cross Channel Express

Services leave from Europa Buscentre in Glengall Street and connect to all major cities and towns across the UK. The service extends to some European destinations including Paris and Amsterdam. Tickets can be obtained at the Travel Centre in the Europa Buscentre (phone 337003), and at any Ulsterbus station or Travel Agent in Northern Ireland.

Ulsterbus Tours

Ulsterbus Tours offer a wide choice of luxury coach holidays in Ireland, north and south, as well as the UK mainland and Europe.

Timetable and Other Information

For any travel information or other type of inquiry, look no further than the Travel Centre in the Europa Buscentre.

The Travel Centre   `13 J10`
Europa Buscentre
Glengall Street
Belfast
BT12 5AH

Telephone : 333000

TAXIS

There are taxi ranks at Central Station, the two main bus stations and the City Hall. Consult the Yellow Pages if you want to book one in advance or try **City Cab** on 242000 or **Fon A Cab** on 233333.

CAR HIRE

Avis: 69/71 Great Victoria Street, Belfast. Phone 240404

Budget: Norwood House, 96-102 Great Victoria Street, Belfast. Phone 230700

McCausland: 21-31 Grosvenor Road, Belfast. Phone 333777

BICYCLE HIRE

Bikes can be hired by the day, weekend or week and the deal usually includes a safety helmet and security lock.

Recycle: 1-5 Albert Square. Phone 313113

WALKING TOURS

In Belfast, you do not have to leave the city to enjoy a walk in the countryside. A trip to one of the city's many parks, see pages 53-57, offers an easy escape from urban living. If you fancy something more substantial in terms of exercise, the Lagan Towpath starts about a mile from the city centre and winds its way south for several miles along the river, passing through beautiful meadows and woodland along the way. Lagan Meadows (p20 J5) are a good starting point for your walk.

If you prefer an organised walking tour, and don't want to venture far from the centre of town, there are several options on offer:

Belfast - The Old Town of 1660-1685 departs from the Tourist Board office on North Street at 2pm on Saturdays from April to October, and takes you on a ninety minute tour which traces the origins of the city, and includes a visit to the Lagan Lookout. Phone 24660 for details.

Belfast City Centre & Laganside Walk departs from the gates of the City Hall at 2pm on Fridays from June to September and takes in the Victorian city centre and Laganside, ending up at the new Waterfront Hall. Phone 491469 for more details.

Belfast City Walk is a conducted tour which leaves from outside Queen's University main gate at 10.30am on Saturdays from June to September. Phone 491469 for more details.

Blackstaff Way is a one hour guided tour of the city centre which departs from the Travelodge on Blackstaff Square every Saturday at 11am from June to September. Phone 333555 for more details.

Bailey's Historical Pub Tours of Belfast cater for those of you who like to make a few pit stops along the way. The tour leaves from Flannigans bar, above the Crown. See page 65 for more details.

Belfast has never been over-endowed with hotels but this situation is being remedied with several recent openings and more new projects in the pipeline as the city begins to reap the dividends of peace.

Availability is not yet a major problem but it is a good idea nevertheless to book your accommodation before you travel. If you have acted on impulse, however, and find yourself in Belfast without a room, Northern Ireland Tourist Board will organise a reservation for a small fee. They have desks at both of Belfast's airports and their main office is at 59 North Street. Credit card bookings can be made by phoning their reservations service on freefone 0800 404050.

A cross section of accommodation is listed below. In an effort to keep things simple, the accommodation has been categorised as 'expensive', 'moderate' or 'budget'. Specific prices are not given as they often vary according to the timing of your stay - most of the selected hotels offer special deals, usually relating to weekend stays. Some of the city's guest houses offer rather more interesting accommodation than many of the hotels and a couple of the better ones are included in the moderate category.

Family-run B&B's form the bedrock of budget accommodation, costing around £20 per person sharing, but most are located in the suburbs of the city. Bookings can be made directly or through the Tourist Board. If you are looking for something cheap but close to the city centre, hostels offer a realistic alternative now that they have shaken off their down-at-heel image. Some have conventional bedrooms but most offer clean and comfortable dorm-style rooms with shared bathrooms. Price normally depends on how many are sharing, but rates are typically around £10 per person per night.

Over the Easter period, and during the summer months from the end of June through to the middle of September, it is possible to book university accommodation at Queen's. This accommodation is well located and costs between £10 and £20 per person per night.

All hotels in Northern Ireland are inspected by the Northern Ireland Tourist Board and are given a star rating, from one to five stars, to reflect the standard of the accommodation and the facilities available. Guest houses, which tend to be less expensive than hotels, are graded by the letters A, B or U. The appropriate rating is listed below after the name of each establishment. All the hotel and guest house accommodation listed provide rooms with en suite bathroom facilities. For a more comprehensive list, contact the Tourist Board on 246609.

Accommodation Prices

Expensive: Expect to pay in the region of £60 to £80 per night per person sharing, including breakfast. Cheaper rates are usually available at weekends.

Moderate: Expect to pay between £30 and £60 per night per person sharing, including breakfast. Once again, cheaper rates are normally available at weekends.

Budget: Most budget accommodation costs between £15 and £30 per night per person sharing.

Northern Ireland Tourist Board's reservation service is available on freefone 0800 404050. For tourist information phone 246609.

EXPENSIVE

CULLODEN HOTEL***
142 Bangor Road, Cutra
Phone 425223 Fax 426777
Formerly a bishop's palace, the Culloden is situated about 15 minutes drive from Belfast city centre and is one of Northern Ireland's most highly rated hotels. The hotel has around 100 ensuite bedrooms and excellent leisure facilities which include a swimming pool, gymnasium, squash and tennis courts.

DUNADRY HOTEL**
2 Islandreagh Drive, Dunadry
Phone (01849) 432474 Fax (01849) 433389
Converted linen mill in tranquil setting just north of Belfast. Leisure facilities include a swimming pool, gymnasium, on site fishing, croquet and bowls.

EUROPA HOTEL**   `13 J10`
Great Victoria Street
Phone 327000 Fax 327800
Belfast's best known hotel, situated close to the city centre and only a short walk from many popular pubs and restaurants. Facilities include the Presidential Suite where Bill and Hillary have stayed, a 20 hour brasserie, bars, restaurant and nightclub.

Historic facade of the McCausland Hotel

HILTON HOTEL***** `14 K10`
Lanyon Place. Phone 277000
New, high-rise, 200 bedroom hotel which occupies a site next door to the Waterfront Hall, overlooking the river.

McCAUSLAND HOTEL**** `14 K11`
Victoria Street. Phone 220200
Another new hotel, but this one is located in a beautifully converted Victorian warehouse, formerly known as the McCausland Building, which is situated close to the city's main shopping area.

MODERATE

THE CRESCENT TOWNHOUSE** `13 J9`
Lower Crescent. Phone 323349
Small hotel situated in an attractive Georgian crescent and benefiting from one of the best restaurants in town. A very good location if you want to be near to some of the best nightlife that Belfast has to offer.

JURY'S BELFAST INN*** `13 J10`
Great Victoria Street. Phone 533500
Located at one end of the city's Golden Mile, Jury's is a successful Irish chain which is currently exporting its format to several British cities. All rooms are available

at a fixed room rate of around £60 per night and can accommodate up to three adults or two adults and two children. Breakfast is not included in the price but all rooms are en suite with colour TV, telephone and tea/coffee making facilities and the hotel has a restaurant and bar.

MALONE GUEST HOUSE (A) `20 H7`
79 Malone Road. Phone 669 565
Simple but well managed guest house in a double-fronted Victorian villa close to Queen's University.

THE OLD INN***
15 Main Street, Crawfordsburn
Phone (01247) 853255
Still partly thatched, the Crawfordsburn is the oldest inn in Ireland. Located in a picturesque village between Belfast and Bangor, the inn has 33 ensuite bedrooms and a popular bar and restaurant.

THE OLD RECTORY(A) `20 H7`
148 Malone Road. Phone 667882
Small but distinctive guest house situated in one of Belfast's most pleasant suburbs.

WELLINGTON PARK HOTEL*** `20 H7`
21 Malone Road
Phone 381111 Fax 665410
Recently extended and refurbished hotel which is located in the heart of university area. The hotel foyer and bars are a busy meeting place on Friday and Saturday nights.

BUDGET

BELFAST INTERNATIONAL YOUTH HOSTEL
22 Donegall Road `13 H9`
Phone 324733 Fax 439699
Modern 38 room youth hostel with 120 beds. Its location close to the university and many of the city's busiest night spots means that all beds are often booked out.

QUEEN'S ELMS HALLS OF RESIDENCE
Malone Road. Phone 381608 `20 H7`
University halls offering Easter and summer accommodation in a pleasant location not far from plenty of city night life.

STRANMILLIS COLLEGE HALLS `20 J7`
Stranmillis Road. Phone 381271
More university accommodation available during the summer months. Once again, pleasantly located and close to plenty of nightlife.

BEACHES

Belfast may be situated on the shores of Belfast Lough but a day at the beach requires a trip outside the city, the most convenient options being Crawfordsburn and Helen's Bay which are both located between Belfast and Bangor and can be reached in around twenty minutes by train or car (see page 47). Northern Ireland's main seaside resorts are Bangor, Newcastle, Portrush and Portstewart.

BELFAST CASTLE 　　6 H18
Off Antrim Road
Phone 776925

Built by the third Marquis of Donegall in 1870 at a time when Queen Victoria's fondness for Balmoral meant that the Scottish Baronial Style was very much in vogue. The marquis's family, the Chichesters, were granted vast tracts of forfeited land during the Plantation of Ulster in 1603. The castle, which was built within a deer park 400 feet up on the slopes of Cave Hill, was donated to the City of Belfast in 1934. A £2m refurbishment was carried out by the city council during the 1980's and facilities now include a heritage centre, antique and craft shop, bar, restaurant, function rooms, and an adventure playground. The grounds of the castle are also open to the public and the relatively gentle climb to the summit of Cave Hill (1,182 feet) is rewarded with a spectacular view over the city and Belfast Lough. There are five caves on the hill and an earthwork called McArts Fort where Wolfe Tone and his United Irishmen took their oaths of fidelity prior to the failed 1798 Rebellion.

BELFAST CITY HALL 　　13 J11
Donegall Square
Phone 320202

Arguably the finest piece of architecture in Belfast, and certainly the city's most recognised landmark, the City Hall is situated in Donegall Square on the site of the former White Linen Hall. Having been granted city status by Queen Victoria in 1888, Belfast decided to respond with a civic building of some magnificence which was intended to reflect the industrial might enjoyed by the city at that time. It was designed by Sir Brumwell Thomas and completed in 1906. The building was constructed in Portland stone in a style somewhat reminiscent of Wren's Saint Paul's Cathedral, with a central copper dome rising 173 feet to dominate the city skyline. A guided tour of the City Hall reveals a sumptuous Italian marble interior which houses many items of interest, including a mural by Belfast artist, John Luke, symbolising the foundation of the city and its principle industries, and the Charter of Belfast granted by James I on 27th April, 1613. Seats

Skateboarders in front of St Anne's Cathedral

in the council chamber are arranged in a similar style to the House of Commons and additional colour is provided by some of the political debate which takes place within. Paintings in the chamber include a portrait of the Earl of Shaftesbury by the eminent Belfast artist, Sir John Lavery. The grounds of the City Hall are laid out in lawns and flower beds which make it a popular place for shoppers and office workers whenever there is a glimmer of afternoon sunshine. Guided tours are conducted October-May, Mon-Sat 2.30pm; June-September Mon-Fri 10.30am, 11.30am & 2.30pm, Saturday 2.30pm. Tours can be booked in advance by phoning 270456.

BELFAST WATERFRONT HALL
See page 58.

BELFAST ZOO 　　4 H20
Off Antrim Road. Phone 776277

Belfast Zoo is situated on a fifty acre site on the slopes of Cave Hill, offering panoramic views over the city and Belfast Lough. The zoo is modern in its outlook, concentrating on the protection of rare and endangered species. Residents include elephants, giraffes and gorillas but one of the highlights is an underwater viewing position which provides a fish eye view of the

Botanic Gardens - an oasis of calm in the heart of the city

sealions and penguins. The zoo is located about five miles north of the city centre and can be reached by Citybus numbers 8, 9, 10 & 45-51. *Opening Times: April-Sept 10am-5pm; Oct-March 10am-3.30pm (2.30pm on Fridays).*

BOTANIC GARDENS   `20 J8`

The Botanic Gardens are situated next door to Queen's University, about one mile south of the city centre and, when the sun comes out, there are few better places to escape the hurly burly of city life. The gardens themselves are beautifully laid out but their best known feature is the Palm House which is the earliest surviving example of a curvilinear glasshouse anywhere in the world. It was completed in 1852 by the Dublin ironfounder, Richard Turner, who went on to build the palm house in London's Kew Gardens. The temperate and tropical plants on display include some carniverous varieties. If the Palm House is not hot enough for you, the gardens also contain the Tropical Ravine where a steamy, artificial climate encourages the growth of orchids, bananas and oranges. The Ravine also houses fish and terrapin ponds. *Opening Times: Mon-Fri 10am-4pm; Sat & Sun 1pm-4pm.*

BELVOIR PARK FOREST   `27 K4`
South Belfast

Headquarters of the Royal Society for the protection of Birds and, not surprisingly, a good location for bird watching. Facilities include a Visitors' Centre. *Opening Times: Mon-Fri 10am-3pm*

CRAFTWORKS   `13 J10`
Bedford Street. Phone 244465

The Craftworks shop displays the very best of Irish design and craftsmanship in the fields of ceramics, jewellery, knitwear and fashion accessories. *Opening Times: Mon-Sat 9.30am-5.30pm (until 8.30pm Thurs)*

CRESCENT ARTS CENTRE
See page 58.

CROWN LIQUOR SALOON
See pages 66 & 71.

CULTURLANN MACADAM O FAICH
See page 58.

CUSTOM HOUSE   `14 K11`
Donegall Quay

Designed by Charles Lanyon, Custom House stands as testimony to the days when Belfast was one of the world's busiest sea ports. The building has undergone a recent refurbishment but the most striking feature remains its sculptured pediment portraying Britannia, Neptune and Mercury looking out over the waterfront.

DUNDONALD INTERNATIONAL ICE BOWL
See page 60.

EAKIN GALLERY   `20 G8`
237 Lisburn Road. Phone 668522

Family run gallery specialising in landscape and still life work by Irish artists. *Opening Times: Mon-Sat 9.30am-5.30pm*

FERNHILL HOUSE: THE PEOPLE'S MUSEUM
Glencairn Road   `8 D13`

Deals with the history of the Shankill area, Home Rule and the two World Wars. *Opening Times: Mon-Sat 10am-4pm; sun 1pm-4pm. Admission charge.*

FENDERESKY GALLERY AT THE CRESCENT
Crescent Arts Centre, 2 University Road   `13 J9`
Phone 242338

Jamshid Mirfenderesky left Iran to study philosophy at Queen's and ended up owning an art gallery which displays work by top names in contemporary Irish art as well as work produced by the up and coming talent.

THE GIANT'S RING   `26 H1`
Neolithic site featuring the Druid's Dolmen, which stands at the centre of a grass-covered, earth rampart which is 600 feet in diameter and dates back some 2,000 years.

GRAND OPERA HOUSE
See page 58.

GROUP THEATRE
See page 58.

HARBOUR COMMISSIONERS OFFICE   `14 K12`
Corporation Square
Built in 1854, the impressive interior is noted for its marble, stained glass and many paintings and sculptures depicting the city's seafaring history. Guided tours are available during *Belfast City Summer Fest*. Phone 554422.

KING'S HALL   `19 F5`
Lisburn Road. Phone 665225.
The King's Hall hosts a wide variety of exhibitions including the Ulster Motor Show and the Ideal Home Exhibition, and it also provides Belfast's largest indoor concert venue where many of the world's leading rock and pop artists have performed in front of 7,000 fans. For many, however, the annual highlight is the Balmoral Show which is hosted by the Royal Ulster Agricultural Society in early May. This is when the country comes to the city, with all manner of farm animals, rare breeds, special displays, show jumping and outdoor and indoor exhibitions. For further details contact the RUAS on 665223.

LAGAN WEIR & LOOKOUT   `14 K11`
Donegall Quay. Phone 315444
The Lagan Weir was completed in 1994 and it has made a huge difference to water quality with salmon returning to the river for the first time in many years. The Lookout houses a visitor centre which contains an interactive exhibition relating to the construction and workings of the weir and the industrial and folk history of the River Lagan. River and harbour boat trips depart from the Lookout. *Opening Times: Apr-Sept Mon-Fri 11am-5pm, Sat 12noon-5pm, Sun2pm-5pm; Oct-Mar Tues-Fri 11am-3.30pm, Sat 1pm-4.30pm, Sun 2pm-4.30pm. Admission charge.*

LINEN HALL LIBRARY   `13 J11`
17 Donegall Square North. Phone 321707
Belfast's oldest library, which was established in 1788 and was originally located in the White Linen Hall before moving to its present location. The library hous-

Queen's University Belfast

es many important collections of Irish interest, including its Political Collection, a comprehensive archive on the recent Troubles. The library is one of the last survivors of the subscription library movement, but a free day pass is available to any visitor who wishes to browse. The reading room is comfortable and you can enjoy a coffee while immersing yourself in periodicals, magazines and the daily newspapers. The librarians are helpful and the prints which line the wall help to create an atmosphere which evokes a bygone era.

LYRIC THEATRE
See page 58.

NORTHERN IRELAND TOURIST BOARD
St Anne's Court, 59 North Street   `13 J11`
Phone 246609
Impressive tourist information office situated between CastleCourt and St Anne's cathedral. Plenty of free info and friendly staff to answer your queries. To book accommodation through the Tourist Board, freephone 0800 404050.

OLD MUSEUM ARTS CENTRE
See page 58.

ORMEAU BATHS GALLERY `13 J10`
Ormeau Avenue
Phone 321402
Belfast's second major gallery after the Ulster Museum, four gallery spaces have been spawned from a former swimming baths which became surplus to the city's requirements. The main focus is on contemporary artists, both international and local. *Opening Times: Tues-Sat 10am-6pm*

PUBLIC RECORDS OFFICE `19 F6`
68 Balmoral Avenue
Phone 225905
The principal repository for records relating to Northern Ireland with documents dating back to the early 17th century. The Public Search Room is a good place to start tracing your Ulster family tree. Open Mon-Fri 9.15am-4.45pm, Thurs until 8.45pm. **The Ulster Historical Foundation** at 12 College Square East may offer further leads if you are trying to trace Belfast ancestors.

QUEEN'S UNIVERSITY OF BELFAST `13 J9`
University Road
One of Charles Lanyon's finest buildings, the main college was modelled on Magdalen College Oxford and was completed in 1849. See page 55.

ROYAL COURTS OF JUSTICE `14 K11`
Chichester Street
The building was a gift to the city from the Westminster Parliament in 1933. Built from Portland stone, it houses four courts with rich interiors of polished marble and woodwork.

ST ANNE'S CATHEDRAL `13 J12`
Donegall Street
No point in rushing a good job - this Church of Ireland Cathedral was begun in 1899 but not finished until the 1980's! The style is Hiberno-Romanesque and the building contains stone from every county in Ireland. See photo on page 53.

ST GEORGE'S MARKET `14 K10`
May Street
Situated opposite the Waterfront Hall, St George's Market was built by Belfast Corporation in 1896 making it one of Ireland's oldest covered markets. At a cost of several million pounds the market has recently been restored to its former architectural glory. The traditional fruit and veg market still takes place every Friday and plans are currently in place to extend trading to other days with the aim of expanding the style and range of merchandise currently available. For more information, phone the Events Co-ordinator on 270386.

ST MALACHY'S CHURCH `14 K9`
Alfred Street
Best known for its fine vaulted ceiling which is similar to the one in Henry VII's chapel in Westminster Abbey.

SINCLAIR SEAMAN'S CHURCH `14 K12`
Corporation Street
Designed by Charles Lanyon in the Venetian style and consecrated in 1853 to serve the spiritual needs of seamen visiting the port of Belfast, this church has become something of a maritime museum. The pulpit is a ship's prow, while the organ sports the port and starboard lights from a Guinness boat from the River Liffey in Dublin and a bell from HMS Hood which was sunk off Jutland in 1916.

SIR THOMAS AND LADY DIXON PARK AND INTERNATIONAL ROSE GARDEN `25 D1`
Upper Malone Road
A Mecca for rose growers with 20,000 blooms scenting the air during Rose Week which run takes place every year in July. Other facilities include a Japanese Garden and a children's play area.

STORMONT `17 U2`
Upper Newtownards Road
Situated about three miles from the city centre, Stormont was home to the Northern Ireland Parliament until 1972 when Direct Rule from Westminster was introduced. Both the building and the setting are impressive: the Portland stone construction has a floor space of 5 acres and it stands at the end of a one mile driveway on an elevated position in 300 acres of parkland which is open to the public. The debating chamber has recently been restored after it was destroyed by fire and, at the time of writing, political power is set to return to Stormont which now houses the new Northern Ireland Assembly. Stormont Castle is next door, but access to both buildings is restricted for security reasons. Citybus numbers 16,17 & 20 from the city centre.

STREAMVALE OPEN DAIRY FARM `17 V9`
Ballyhanwood Road
Phone 483244
Working farm where you can watch the dairy herd being milked or bottle-feed a lamb. Facilities include a nature trail, pony rides, picnic area, shop and cafe. *Opening Times: Feb-May & Sept-Oct Wed,Sat & Sun 2pm-6pm; July-Aug Mon-Sun 10.30-6pm*

TOM CALDWELL GALLERY `13 J9`
Bradbury Place
Phone 323226

A leading figure on the local arts scene, Tom Caldwell displays the work of established Irish painters as well as talented newcomers in a gallery which occupies the same building as his interesting furniture shop.

ULSTER HALL `13 J10`
Bedford Street
Phone 323900

The Ulster Hall is a 19th century building which houses the magnificent Mulholland Organ. The Ulster Orchestra still give performances in the Hall which is also used for a wide range of other concerts and recitals, from classical to rock and pop.

ULSTER FOLK & TRANSPORT MUSEUM
On the A2, Belfast to Bangor Road
Phone 428428

Situated just outside Belfast at Cultra, this is a museum of two complementary halves. The Folk Museum gives a unique insight into Ulster life around the turn of the century by reconstructing an ever-increasing number of houses, workshops, mills, shops, schools, churches and other public buildings which have been removed from all parts of the province and rebuilt stone by stone within the rural setting of the museum, which overlooks Belfast Lough. Inside most of the buildings you will find a blazing peat fire and a friendly and informative attendant. The centre piece of the Transport Museum is the Irish Railway Collection which is housed within a huge new gallery. Other galleries display a diverse range of exhibits which include early Ulster-built planes and motorbikes, a De Lorean motor car assembled in Belfast in 1982, and an exhibition dedicated to the Titanic, which was built in Belfast in 1912 and sank on her maiden voyage to New York with the loss of 1,500 lives. The museum can be reached by catching a bus or train heading from Belfast to Bangor. Get off at Cultra.

ULSTER MUSEUM `20 J8`
Botanic Gardens
Phone 383000

Situated about a mile south of the city centre, Northern Ireland's national museum houses fascinating collections of fine and decorative art, antiquities, local history and natural sciences. Displays include the award-winning *Early Ireland* gallery, *Treasures of the Armada* and the newly refurbished temporary exhibition gallery. The annual programme includes lectures, films and weekend activities. *Opening Times: Mon-*

Ulster Museum's temporary exhibition gallery

Fri 10am-5pm; Sat 1pm -5pm; Sun 2pm-5pm. Admission is free. Citybus number 69.

ULSTER WEAVERS'DISPLAY CENTRE `22 P7`
Montgomery Road.
Phone 404236

Guided tours of this modern linen weaving factory take place on a daily basis but prior arrangement is required. Facilities include a cafe and a gift shop stocked with Irish craftware. *Opening Times: Mon-Sat 9.30am-5pm*

THE WORKSHOPS COLLECTIVE FOR ARTS & CRAFTS `13 J9`
1A Lawrence Street.
Phone 200707

Situated in 19th century stables in the heart of the university area, the Workshops Collective is a busy haven of local artists and bustling workshops. The Collective's showroom stages Winter and Summer exhibitions which include demonstrations and guided tours. The showroom remains open all year, displaying a diverse range of crafts, furniture and art. *Opening Times: Mon-Fri 10am-6pm, Sat 11am-4pm, Sun by prior arrangement.*

Belfast, like the rest of Ireland, is proud of its artistic tradition and the arts have been going from strength to strength in recent years thanks to considerable investment in new venues, and continuing financial support from public and private sectors.

The opening of Belfast's Waterfront Hall in 1997 added a new jewel to the city's entertainment crown but the cultural highlight of the year undoubtedly remains the **Belfast Festival at Queen's** which normally runs for two to three weeks in November. This is a world class festival of culture which attracts many international artists from the world of theatre, dance, music and comedy who perform at venues in and around Queen's University.

If you are planning a night out at the theatre, cinema or a performance of live music or comedy, the **What's On** section of the **Belfast Telegraph** is a good place to start.

THEATRES

BELFAST WATERFRONT HALL `14 K11`
Lanyon Place

When Belfast Waterfront Hall opened its doors in January 1997, it marked the completion of the most significant civic building to be built in Belfast since the City Hall was completed in 1906. In common with many other major public buildings, the development attracted its fair share of controversy, with the final cost exceeding £30m, this sum being funded by Belfast City Council with support from Laganside Corporation and the European Union. The Waterfront Hall is seen by many as a landmark project which will reflect Belfast's renewed self-confidence, and the end result is certainly impressive. The main auditorium seats 2,235 and has already hosted major symphony concerts and recitals as well as many rock and pop performances. The 400-seat BT studio provides state of the art conference facilities and also plays host to dance and drama performances by local and visiting companies. Even if you are not attending a performance, the Waterfront Hall is worth visiting for the attractive views which can be enjoyed from the glass fronted bar and restaurant. For box office and credit card bookings phone 334455. For information and reservations phone 334400.

CRESCENT ARTS CENTRE `13 J9`
2-4 University Road

Converted Victorian school which hosts workshops in all kinds of dance, circus, music and other artistic skills as well as staging regular studio performances and exhibitions. Phone 242338.

CULTURLANN MACADAM O FAICH `12 F10`
216 Falls Road

Irish language arts centre which stages most of its theatrical productions in Irish although simultaneous translations are usually available to those people with little or no understanding of the language. Phone 239303.

GRAND OPERA HOUSE `13 J10`
Great Victoria Street

The Grand Opera House is a monument to the extravagance of Victorian theatre designer, Robert Matcham. The turrets and curlicues which make up the facade reflect an Eastern influence which is also evident inside where sculpted elephants support the boxes and the lavishly painted ceiling. Although the first opening curtain was in 1895, the Victorian splendour owes much to painstaking restoration carried out in more recent times following serious bomb damage. The Opera House is home to Opera Northern Ireland but it is much more than a venue for opera - it stages a wide variety of theatre, music, dance, comedy, and even pantomime. There are special facilities for wheelchair users and an induction loop system relays non-musical performances to hearing aid users. Phone the box office on 241919.

GROUP THEATRE `13 J10`
Bedford Street

The Group Theatre forms part of the Ulster Hall complex which is operated by Belfast City Council. The theatre seats 240 and stages a large number of productions, performed mainly by local dramatic societies. Phone the box office on 329685.

LYRIC THEATRE `20 J7`
55 Ridgeway Street

Founded by Mary O'Malley in the 1950's, the Lyric is Northern Ireland's only repertory theatre, presenting a broad range of classical and contemporary plays with a particular emphasis on Irish work. The theatre aims to fulfil a broad role, offering fifty weeks a year of varied programming ranging from live music, dance and comedy events to co-productions with local theatre companies and the best of Irish theatre. Situated on the banks of the Lagan in the heart of Stranmillis village, the theatre is only two miles from the city centre on a major Citybus route. Access is available for patrons with special needs and the auditorium is equipped with a loop induction system. Ph 381081 for the box office.

OLD MUSEUM ARTS CENTRE
7 College Square North `13 J11`

Intimate theatre space and gallery with an avant-garde

artistic policy. Productions include drama, dance and poetry and there are regular workshops and exhibitions of art and photographs. Phone 233332.

OPERA

Opera Northern Ireland has co-operated very successfully with the Ulster Orchestra to stage some very lavish productions during their spring and summer seasons at the Grand Opera House, and their efforts have been rewarded with national critical acclaim.

COMEDY

Belfast is usually included on the touring schedule of the major comedy acts who tend to play the main theatrical venues such as the Waterfront Hall and the Grand Opera House. Come November, the Belfast Festival at Queen's attracts a plethora of comedy acts to town including many of the critical successes seen a few weeks earlier at the Edinburgh Fringe.

Several Belfast pubs have staged live comedy but Tuesday night at the Empire on Botanic Avenue is the mainstay, made famous by local boy made good, Paddy Kielty who acted as compere for many years. The evening usually showcases a combination of local talent and some bigger fish drawn from comedy circuits in London and Dublin. A good laugh is usually guaranteed.

CINEMA

The Northern Ireland Film Commission was set up in 1997 to promote Northern Ireland as a potential location for film makers. Several movies have been made locally in recent years including Divorcing Jack and Titanic Town.

For many years the number of Belfast cinemas seemed to be in inexorable decline, but the advent of the multiplex has reversed this trend and there are now dozens of screens to choose from around the city. Most concentrate on the mainstream Hollywood releases and, as a consequence, many cinemas end up showing the same film. **The Queen's Film Theatre** (University Mews, off Botanic Avenue, phone 244857) is the main exception to this rule, catering to followers of European cinema as well as screening many cult classics.

Virgin's 10 screen cinema on the Dublin Road hosts **Cinemagic,** an annual film festival which runs for a week, usually in December.

MUSIC

Belfast is steeped in musical tradition, with the likes of

The Crescent Arts Centre & Fenderesky Gallery

Van Morrison and James Galway among its famous sons. The city is regularly included on the itinerary of these and countless other celebrated international artists and entertainers.

For lovers of classical music, the Ulster Orchestra performs a series of concerts throughout the year at the Ulster Hall and at the Waterfront Hall. The orchestra continues to grow in reputation, both at home and abroad, and has performed several times at the Henry Wood Promenade Concerts in London's Royal Albert Hall. It also enjoys a successful relationship with Opera Northern Ireland which stages its productions at the Grand Opera House. For details of concerts and recordings, contact the ticket office on 668798.

It will come as no surprise to learn that Belfast pubs provide the main platform for local bands and musicians. There are dozens of such venues and many of them are listed in the Pubs section on pages 65-72. A good choice of rock, jazz, folk and blues is usually on offer. Most of the major rock and pop concerts in Belfast take place at either the King's Hall or the Waterfront Hall, but Botanic Gardens has also been used for several large outdoor concerts in recent years, the largest of which was a widely acclaimed performance by U2. For lovers of jazz, the annual highlight is the Holywood International Jazz Festival which usually takes place in June and manages to attract some famous names. Once again, the What's On section of the Belfast Telegraph and the Big Buzz are good places to find out what's on where and when.

Northern Ireland punches a lot more than its weight when it comes to sport. Facilities tend to be good considering the size of population, and the opportunity exists to participate in most sporting activities. The Sports Council is a useful source of information - phone 381222.

ATHLETICS

International athletics meetings are held at the Mary Peters Track which is in the Malone Playing Fields, just off the Upper Malone Road. The track is in the care of the City Council and is available for public use. Major annual events include the World Cross-Country Championships which usually take place in March and the Belfast Marathon which is normally staged in May.

ICE SKATING

Dundonald International Ice Bowl   `17 V9`
111 Old Dundonald Road.
Phone 482611
The Ice Bowl boasts an Olympic sized rink which is used for ice hockey as well as skating. Lessons are available from highly trained resident instructors. Other facilities on site include 30 lanes of ten pin bowling, Indiana Land, a jungle themed play area for children, and Megazone.

FOOTBALL

The English Premiership attracts much more interest locally than the domestic football programme, but several Belfast teams play in the Irish League, including Linfield who play at Windsor Park, Glentoran who play at the Oval on Parkgate Drive, Cliftonville who play at Solitude on Cliftonville Street, and Crusaders who play at Seaview on Saint Vincent Street. Most league matches are played on Saturdays.

On the international front, Northern Ireland have been going through a lean spell since qualifying for two World Cups during the 1980's. International matches are played at Windsor Park. The Irish Football League can be contacted on 242888.

GAELIC GAMES

The main venue for watching Gaelic football and hurling is Roger Casement Park on the Andersonstown Road. The nine counties of Ulster compete in the Ulster Championships with the winner going on to compete for a place in the all Ireland finals which are played at Croke Park in Dublin in September each year. The Ulster Council of the Gaelic Athletic Association can be contacted on 383815.

GOLF

Unlike many other countries, golf is not seen as an elitist game in Ireland. Northern Ireland is lucky enough to have two of the finest links courses in the world at Royal Portrush, which has staged the British Open, and Royal County Down which enjoys a breathtaking setting where the mountains of Mourne sweep down to the sea.

Malone Golf Club in Belfast is one of the best parkland courses in Ireland and Belvoir Park gives Malone a good run for its money. There are courses to suit players of all abilities and green fees tend not to be prohibitively expensive, especially at the municipal courses. A full list is available in the Yellow Pages, but a few of the better courses in and around Belfast are listed below. All are private clubs but visitors are welcome, especially during the week, although it is advisable to phone beforehand.

If you want to see how the game really should be played, take a trip to the Irish Open which is one of the leading tournaments on the European Tour, attracting many of the world's top players. The venue changes, as does the timing, but the event is normally staged in early July.

Balmoral Golf Club   `19 E5`
518 Lisburn Road. Phone 667747
6,177 yards. Par 69

Belvoir Park Golf Club   `27 L5`
73 Church Road, Newtownbreda.
Phone 646714
6,476 yards. Par 71

Knock Golf Club   `17 V11`
Upper Newtownards Road. Phone 483825
6,407 yards. Par 70

Malone Golf Club   `25 E2`
240 Upper Malone Road. Phone 614917
6,656 yards. Par 71

Shandon Park Golf Club   `16 R9`
73 Shandon Park. Phone797859
6011 yards. Par 70

New Forge Lane Golf Centre   `26 H4`
22 New Forge Lane
Phone 683174.
Driving range with 26 floodlit bays open until 10pm every day.

GYMNASIUMS

It is a partly a legacy of the divisions brought about by the Troubles, but Belfast is endowed with more public leisure centres than you are likely to find anywhere else of a similar size in the world. There are more than a dozen dotted around the city (see Yellow Pages for a full list), and most enjoy the benefits of hi tech fitness equipment, and many have their own swimming pool, sauna & solarium, squash courts, and football pitches.

Maysfield Leisure Centre on East Bridge Street, next door to Central Railway Station, is the most centrally located of the council run centres. Facilities there include indoor sports halls, swimming pool, hi-tech fitness room, 2 squash courts, sauna, solarium, and an outdoor 5-a-side pitch. Phone 241633 for more details.

HORSES

Ireland is famous throughout the world for producing thoroughbred race horses and Northern Ireland has two courses where you can go along and enjoy a flutter. The annual highlights in the racing calendar are the Ulster Harp National which is run at Downpatrick in March, and the Ulster Harp Derby, which is a more fashionable affair, run at Down Royal, near Lisburn, in July. Both courses stage other meetings during the year.

If you prefer riding horses to betting on them, **Lagan Valley Equestrian Centre** is conveniently located at 170 Malone Road. Facilities include an indoor and outdoor arena as well as cross country riding. Phone 614853 for more details.

RUGBY

Lansdowne Road in Dublin is the headquarters of the Irish Rugby Football Union and the home venue for all of Ireland's international matches. The highlight of the year is the Six Nations Championship which takes place from January to March when Ireland take on England, Scotland, Wales, France and Italy. Thousands of away fans invade Dublin for what is a great social occasion and, despite a conspicuous lack of Irish success in recent years, tickets are very difficult to acquire.

Ravenhill Stadium is the HQ of the Ulster branch of the union, and 1999 will long be remembered for Ulster's victory in the European Cup. For further details phone the Irish Rugby Football Union on 649141.

SKIING

Ireland may not be renowned for its achievements in the Winter Olympics but it is possible to hone your skiing, snowboarding and tobogganing technique at an artificial slope on the outskirts of town. Instruction is available and use of the facilities currently costs £6 per hour.

Ski Mount Ober
Ballymaconaghy Road, Knockracken, Belfast 8. Phone 792108.

SWIMMING

As mentioned earlier, the city is very well off when it comes to swimming pools. A few of the main ones are listed below:

Grove Leisure Centre `10 K14`
York Road. Telephone 351599
Gala Pool - 25 x 12.8m - with capacity for 800 spectators.

Maysfield Leisure Centre `14 K10`
East Bridge Street. Telephone 241633
25m Swimming Pool

Olympia Leisure Centre `19 F7`
Boucher Road. Telephone 233369
25m Swimming Pool

Shankill Leisure Centre `13 G12`
Shankill Road. Telephone 241434
Free Form Swimming Pool with Wavemaker

TEN PIN BOWLING

Dundonald International Ice Bowl `17 V9`
111 Old Dundonald Road. Phone482611
30 lanes.

Belfast Superbowl `13 J10`
4 Clarence Street West. Phone 331446
20 lanes.

TENNIS

Since most clubs are privately run for the benefit of their members and guests, the most realistic option is a game at one of the city's leisure centres. The best public facility is the **Belfast Indoor Tennis Arena** which has 4 indoor courts and is situated in Ormeau Park, off the Ormeau Embankment. Phone 458024.

PARKING

The problems generally associated with finding a city centre parking space seem to have largely disappeared in Belfast. In addition to the 1600 spaces provided by CastleCourt, there are several other car parks in the centre of town, most notably High Street Car Park.

A 'Pay & Display' system operates to the south of the City Hall where there are several hundred on-street parking spaces where a couple of hours parking will cost around £2.

The central location of the city's two main bus stations, and the opening of a new train station on Great Victoria Street, means that many shoppers heading for Belfast now can choose to leave their car at home.

SHOPS

Growing up in Belfast in the '70s and early 80's was pretty depressing and, for an avid shopper, a tiresome, exasperating and even humiliating experience with limited choice and frequent body searches. The more peaceful '90's have awakened the consumer in us all with a huge expansion in outlets to meet all needs and aspirations. The emphasis is on high quality, branded goods for the discerning professional with a bit of dosh to spend, although Ulster financial canniness demands both fashion *and* quality.

Women's and Men's Fashion

Marks and Spencer in Donegall Place has been the stalwart, both of fashion and food retailing, throughout Belfast's recent Troubles. Other British multiples have recently congregated around the same area with Next and Principles in the old Robinson & Cleaver building and, Top Shop, Body Shop, Monsoon and the Levi's Store nearby. The new Karen Millen store, with bright ultra fashionable womanswear, is the latest addition. Further down sees shoe shop, Nine West, and the old Bank Buildings has long since been converted into a branch of Primark, stocking low price fashion in a higglety pigglety store with occasional gems. Eamon Holmes was once a manager here.

Around Castle Lane and Cornmarket there are lower priced stores such as BHS, River Island, Littlewoods, and the funkiest shoe shop in town, DV8. A major addition to the retail scene is the CastleCourt Centre on Royal Avenue with more than 70 shops in a modern, purpose built, glass-fronted structure which houses good old reliables such as Debenham's, Dorothy Perkins, Laura Ashley, Benetton, Dolcis, Burton, Warehouse, FCUK, and the rummager's paradise, the occasionally fantastic TK Maxx.

A major gap in Belfast's repertoire is a decent Dunne's Stores in the city centre. Ireland's answer to M&S may not achieve the same retailing standards, but often a good buy such as linen suits will be seen on the backs of those who shudder at the words 'chain store'.

The young and trendy can find slinky club wear in Miss Selfridge's and Morgan in Castlecourt, and Kookai on Castle Lane.

The area behind Donegall Place is known as the Fountain area and has a number of smaller shops such as Earth Works, The Penshop, Athletic Stores and *the* original delicatessen - Sawers, still bringing unusual goodies to the Irish palate despite the influx of British supermarket chains. There are several good eateries on Fountain Street if your feet and credit card need a rest. See Alto's, Cafe Poirot, and Roscoff Cafe on pages 73-80).

Further along in Upper Queen Street the Spires Mall in the old Presbyterian building offers a new type of religion - retail therapy. Carters is one of the original designer shops for both sexes, for those whose clothes whisper their price label in discreet tones of Armani, Mani, Victor Victoria, Ralph Lauren etc. Funky and brash Diesel is a welcome addition to the other shops in this corner, with one of the best, occasionally controversial, style magazine advertisement campaigns. Nearby, The Bureau has also featured in the same magazines for their attempts to clothe Belfast man in Paul Smith and the like. A small woman's selection is also available. Roger in Wellington Place has a stock of chic, sophistication in the form of classic Marella, Max Mara and the like. Propaganda screams,' if you've got it flaunt it!', in D&G, Destroy and adopted Irish designer, John Rocha.

Moving smoothly, if not painlessly, down Great Victoria Street, Estrasse, stockists of Escada as well as the likes of Victor Victoria, attracts clientele from all over Northern Ireland, while much further down Parks will kit men and women out in urban sports and utility wear, in glass fronted surroundings to make sure that you know you are in the place to be seen, and you can linger with a cup of coffee, if there is any chance of being missed.

Behind in Bedford Street a welcome addition has been the Glasshouse, who are willing to make you slaver and drool over the Nicole Fahri, D&G, Paul Smith and Rifat Ozbeck collections. Still recovering from the gaffe of saying that Irish woman don't have style, Paul Costello's shop in Bradbury Place stock the original and diffusion line of classic, well cut, designer clothes in natural fabrics. Seemingly Princess Di

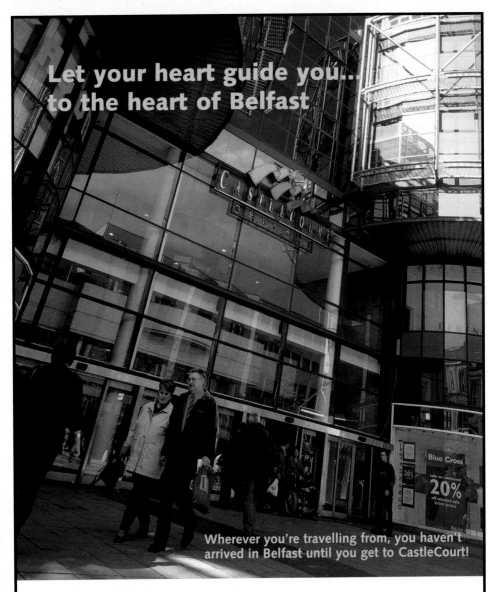

Let your heart guide you...
to the heart of Belfast

Blue Cross
take an additional
20%
off selected sale
ticket prices

Wherever you're travelling from, you haven't
arrived in Belfast until you get to CastleCourt!

Over 70 World-Class Shops and Services

CASTLE COURT
THE HEART OF BELFAST

was a fan, if that is any accolade. Bargains can be found in the factory shop in Dungannon (and the outlet store in Cheshire). Next door is Brazil, favoured by the In Wear and Part II thirtysomethings. Outhouse supplies designer gear such as Paul Smith, and Rio will kit the man out in Matinique and John Rocha Jeans.

The Lisburn Road now has a little group of shops catering to the BT9 set. The leader of the pack, Coral, is still going, selling Armani and Kenzo amongst other desirable labels. Chameleon at number 585 may be small but it you are looking for Betty Jackson, and Fenn, Wright and Mason, this is the place. The minimalist Panache at number 723 will make sure you step out in style in Maxmara, Marella, Sportmax, English Eccentric and last word for understated chic of Donna Karan Signature. Harper will ensure your outfit is accessorised with a stylish bag. The feet of Ulster have been crying out for fashion, and help is on hand in the form of Rojo. The ultimate fashion victim's shop stocks the ultimate label, Prada.

Interiors

Ikea-owned Habitat, in the old Anderson & Mac Auley building in Donegall Place, provides modern classics for the burgeoning number of home owners.

A shrine to modern glassware, ceramics, and kitchenware, Equinox's extensive range of Alessi, and Rosenthal form the basis of many a wedding list in 321 Howard Street. The cafe is pretty cool as well.

Batik on Adelaide Street stocks unusual, creative and desirable home furnishings. Tom Jones in CastleCourt has a more traditional style. Tyrone crystal may not have the same cachet as Waterford but is good quality. The famous Belleek china also makes a welcome pressie.

More contemporary local craftware from a variety of artists is on sale through Craftworks in Bedford Street. The Natural Interior on the Dublin Road is a branch of the successful Dublin-based company. Tom Caldwell's on Bradbury Place is still going and keeping up with the best of modern design classics as well as contemporary art. He likes to think of it as a gallery rather than a shop, but ignoring some of the pompous twaddle this actually results in a great, really great, place to browse, buy, plagiarize ideas, and create a home to die for.

Fulton's in Boucher Retail Park sounds unprepossessing, but worth the trail to Boucher Crescent to fill your home with the best. Little joy for bargain hunters though.

To prove Belfast is not the be all and end all, Ballymena rates a mention for Store, Store. Urban dwellers who get asthma when exposed to country air beat their way to 12 Broadway Avenue for designer furniture, interiors, the deli, and to pose in the first floor cafe. The perfect one stop life style shop.

Jewellery

Fred Malcolm's on Chichester Street is a superb, old fashioned, discreet jewellery store with pleasant, friendly staff and, although expensive, you are paying for quality. Sinclair Rainey on Howard Street, has stylish jewellery, but the in- place for that individual, one-off, wedding ring and other pieces of distinctive jewellery is still The Steensons in Bedford Street, although some showier items have crept in more recently. There aren't many reasons to go to Stroke City (Derry/Londonderry to the Gerry Anderson free), but Thomas the Goldsmith on 7 Pump Street is definitely one for contemporary young designs . If you fancy a bite afterwards, Gravy comes highly recommended.

Books

Waterstone's on Royal Avenue, with a wide ranging local section, Dillons in Fountain Street, and Easons (CastleCourt and Ann Street are the main city centre branches) are all excellent, as is the Queen's University Bookshop, and Edco on Jordanstown campus and 47 Queen Street. No shortage of browsing possibilities

Music

HMV in Donegall Arcade, Virgin in CastleCourt (with the Virgin Ticketshop), and Our Price on Donegall Place churn out mega deals on all sorts of music, but don't forget the locals, Golden Discs on Donegall Place, and the Gramophone Shop on Donegall Square North. Good Vibrations, now on Howard Street, justly claims to be Belfast's most famous record shop. Koinonia in Pottinger's Entry provides a wide ranging mail order service and Street Dance Records, unsurprisingly, specialises in dance music in Arthur Lane.

Markets

St. George's market is great for fresh fruit, flowers, vegetables and local banter, and following a multi million pound redevelopment looks set to expand its range with some new market days in the pipeline.

For the opinions expressed above, thanks go to the Coyle sisters whose single minded devotion to flexing their plastic has helped to put Belfast back on the retailing map.

It seems that wherever you go in the world these days, an Irish pub is rarely far away. Ireland rightly has a reputation for great pubs and Belfast certainly upholds this tradition. The pub represents the heart and soul of the city's social life and there are hundreds to choose from. Belfast may have had more than its fair share of trouble over the years but its citizens have never lost their appetite for ' a good night's *craic*' which goes a long way to explaining the popularity and the appeal of the city's pubs.

There are many historic pubs dotted around the city centre, and a growing number of modern ones which reflect the growing trend for cafe bars. It is difficult in many cases to distinguish between pubs, clubs and bars as many of Belfast's watering holes fit comfortably into all three categories. The list below tries to point you in the direction of some of the best but, if you feel strongly that any have been wrongly included or unfairly omitted, feel free to let us know (see page 2 for contact details).

Most of the pubs listed serve food and many stage live music. To find out who is playing when and where, pick up a copy of **The Big List,** a free guide to what's on which is published every fortnight and is available in many shops, cafes and venues around town. Alternatively, look in the **What's On** section of the **Belfast Telegraph** or invest £1.95 in a copy of **The Big Buzz,** a locally based entertainment magazine which focuses heavily on music and the club scene.

The list below is NOT broken into categories as so many of Belfast's bars and clubs fall into more than one bracket. Many bars have their own nightclub where you can drink and dance until 1am, and much later in some cases. Opening hours have also been omitted due to the relaxed nature of the licensing laws in Belfast. Extensions are frequently applied to normal opening times which are 11.30am to 11pm Monday to Saturday, and 12noon to 10pm on Sundays. Half an hour drinking up time is allowed after these hours.

Beer consumption is dominated by two major brewers, Guinness and Bass, although a local real ale alternative is provided by Hilden which is brewed in Lisburn. If spirits are your favourite tipple, it is well worth noting that Northern Ireland measures are 40% bigger than those served in English pubs!

There are good pubs all over Belfast but it is fair to say that the bulk of the really popular ones are located in the south of the city, especially around the university area. This phenomenon gave rise to the phrase, 'Belfast's Golden Mile', an area which runs south from Great Victoria Street to the bottom of the

Malone Road. This stretch still contains many of the city's best bars and restaurants but the centre of gravity is continually shifting as areas such as the Lisburn Road and the docks stake their claim to a slice of the action..

Finally, if you like to keep on the move but you aren't sure where you are going, you might like to try an organised pub crawl. **Bailey's Historical Pub Tours of Belfast** do what the title implies, starting at Flannigan's Bar which is situated above the Crown. The entrance is on Amelia Street. Tours run June & August every Tuesday at 7pm, Friday at 5.30pm, and Saturday at 4pm; May, July & September every Friday at 5.30pm and Saturday at 4pm. Group tours can be booked all year round. Phone 681278 for further information.

If you would rather organise your own pub crawl, then feel free to work your way through the list below!

AUNTY ANNIE'S `13 J10`
Dublin Road
Aunty Annie's proves the old adage that when it comes to property the three most important aspects are location, location and location. This is one of those theme bars where it's difficult to guess what the theme might be, but it's in the right place to attract a passing crowd from nearby cinemas and restaurants. It's a pleasant bar as it is but, once it sorts out its identity crisis, it will surely do even better.

BAR 12 `13 J9`
13 Lower Crescent
Phone 323349
A bar which sits comfortably in this very attractive Georgian crescent. The design has a slightly colonial feel with its ceiling fans and leather armchairs which are strong contenders for most comfortable in Ireland. All in all a very pleasant environment in which to practise the art of conversation!

BENEDICT'S `13 J9`
7-21 Bradbury Place
Phone 591999
One of a new breed of Belfast super pubs, although this one has been developed in conjunction with a hotel. Much of the gothic style interior seems to have come via an architectural salvage yard judging by the abundance of carved wood and stained glass. This is a large bar to fill but its location and a weekly programme of musical events usually guarantees a brisk trade.

The Crescent Townhouse and Bar 12 on Lower Crescent

BITTLES `14 K11`
103 Victoria Street
Phone 311088
Characterful, city centre pub which displays some interesting local art but is best known as a good spot to enjoy some Ulster home cooking come lunchtime.

BOB'S `20 G8`
Russell Court Complex
52/54 Lisburn Road
Phone 332526
Recently refurbished bar which is located in a former hotel across the road from the City Hospital. The interior is spacious and comfortable and it attracts a good lunchtime trade, but the main attraction comes later in the evening when a youthful clientele converge for the various club nights hosted throughout the week next door at **Storm**.

BOTANIC INN `20 H7`
23 Malone Road
Phone 660460
The Bot remains a Belfast institution despite being totally rebuilt a few years ago. Its location close to Queen's University guarantees a busy bar throughout the day and night. The new look Bot is a blend of traditional and modern styles which attracts a wide cross section of customers, young and not so young, students and professionals. A good place to watch live football on a big screen. Live music and disco upstairs.

CHELSEA WINE BAR `20 G8`
346 Lisburn Road. Phone 687177
The Chelsea is a bit of a standard bearer for the rejuvenation of the Lisburn Road, attracting a slightly older, well heeled crowd who tend to pack the place out most of the time. Upstairs is slightly less hectic than downstairs where it can be a bit difficult getting to the bar at times. The decor is light and sunny throughout and upstairs has a conservatory feel to it. The drinks menu includes a list of twenty wines, a range of cocktails and numerous draught and bottled beers, and food is served throughout the day and night.

THE CROWN BAR `13 J10`
46 Great Victoria Street. Phone 249476
More has been written about this pub than any other in Belfast, and deservedly so. The Crown is such an architectural gem that it is in the care of the National Trust. The pub dates from 1826 but the opulent decor for which it is famed is attributable to the skills of Italian craftsmen who came to Belfast much later to work on the famous liners being built at Harland & Wolf shipyard. The result is an unrivalled example of a High Victorian Gin Palace with lots of stained glass, mosaic tiling and intricate wood carving. There are ten wooden snugs, somewhat reminiscent of old railway compartments, with some delightful attention to detail such as gas lighting and an original Victorian bell system for summoning service. More tourists visit this pub than any other in Belfast but the clientele manages to remain fairly local. If you are visiting from outside Ireland and find yourself ordering your first ever pint of Guinness, you might as well go the whole hog and and try a bowl of their excellent Irish stew. You can even check the bar out via its web camera which can be accessed through the Belfast Telegraph web site..

CUTTER'S WHARF `20 J6`
Lockview Road
Phone 662501
A very welcome addition to fashionable Stranmillis, an area strangely devoid of pubs, the Cutter's Wharf was built only a few years ago on the edge of the River Lagan. One of the few Belfast pubs to offer the

fair weather drinker the chance to sip something cool out of doors, the interior has been designed along the lines of a boat house - stone flagged floors and lots of bare wooden beams. Cutters has lost out a bit recently to the likes of McHughs, the Chelsea and the Fly, but it remains crowded most days of the week, especially so at weekends. Jazz brunches are a popular feature on Sundays, and the restaurant upstairs is well rated.

DEER'S HEAD `13 J11`
1 Lower Garfield Street
Phone 239163
If you have just visited the Northern Ireland Tourist Board office in North Street, a stroll across the road will bring you to the Deer's Head where you can digest the tourist info in attractive surroundings and plan your itinerary over a quiet pint. Lunchtime trade is usually brisk given its proximity to CastleCourt and the city's main shopping area.

DEMPSEY'S TERRACE `13 J10`
43 Dublin Road
Phone 234000
A combination of various themed bars, restaurant and nightclub (**The Loft**) this large complex was at the forefront of revitalising Belfast nightlife back in the 1980's. A popular spot for late night drinking and dancing. Door policy is over 23, no jeans, and no tattoos on display (especially if they aren't spelled right).

DUKE OF YORK `13 J11`
11 Commercial Court
Phone 241062
One of the oldest pubs in Belfast, the Duke of York is tucked away up a side street close to St Anne's Cathedral. The pub has been totally refurbished but it retains its old world charm. Live music several nights a week helps to pull in the customers after dark.

THE EDGE `14 L11`
Mays Meadow
Phone 322000
It's early days but this new riverside pub and restaurant may struggle at times to reach 'full steam ahead' due to its slightly isolated location. Both the exterior and interior have their good points but overall the development doesn't seem to have lived up to its full potential. Inside is a bit too familiar, looking as if it's had a makeover from the Changing Rooms team, and lacking some of the imaginative touches which one might expect for two million quid. Everything is certainly on a grand scale, however, and the series of

Can you remember your first pint?

double doors opening out onto a riverside sun deck will certainly be a crowd pleaser on a warm summers day.

THE EGLANTINE INN `20 H7`
32 Malone Road
Phone 381994
Many bars in Belfast are spoken of in reference to another. So it is with the Egg, the Bot and the Welly Park which form a sort of drinkers' Bermuda Triangle at the bottom end of the Malone Road, close to Queen's University. All three are among the busiest bars in town and each has been totally rebuilt in recent years. The Egg has abandoned its traditional roots and opted instead for a modern cafe bar look. A cast iron staircase features prominently throughout all three floors, and racks of wine now dominate behind the bar although beer remains the favourite tipple of the predominantly youthful clientele. Decent pub grub is on offer, and there are regular disco nights upstairs.

THE ELMS `13 J9`
36 University Road
Phone 322106
Busy pub near to Queen's University which caters to the local student population with a regular diet of

Re-stocking the bar at the Fly

live music.

EMPIRE   `13 J9`
42 Botanic Avenue
Phone 328110
It was a long time in coming but it was the Empire that introduced live comedy to Belfast's pubs. Local boy made good, Paddy Kielty, used to compere the show-case of talent which comes from near and far every Tuesday night during term time. Get there early if you want a table, but bear in mind that you might be drinking for a couple of hours before you see the first act. This seems to affect people in one of two ways: either they suddenly find that everything in life is unbeliev ably funny, or they discover that they were born to heckle. Comedy is staged both downstairs, and musical events are staged both downstairs and upstairs in the Empire Music Hall which is one of the most impressive venues in town.

ERRIGLE INN   `21 K8`
312-320 Ormeau Road
Phone 641410
The Errigle is an Ormeau Road stalwart which has

enjoyed unbroken popularity for many years. Despite a recent facelift, the downstairs bar retains a rather timeless air which makes it a good place to pull up a chair and forget about the world outside. The Errigle is in fact a complex of bars with a strong emphasis on live music which helps to broaden its appeal.

EUROPA HOTEL   `13 J10`
Great Victoria Street
Phone 327000
Lively public bar on the ground floor and quieter lounge bar on the first floor where a pianist plays nightly. The hotel's nightclub, Paradise Lost, caters to a slightly older crowd than many of other night spots in town. Entrance on Glengall Street.

THE FLY   `13 J9`
5-6 Lower Crescent
Phone 235666
Who said that size doesn't matter? Since it recently extended into next door the Fly is unrecognisable, and it is currently the hottest bar in town. Located in an attractive Georgian crescent, the interior is dominated by a Gaudi-esque spiral staircase which winds its way through three floors. The ground floor and first floor bars have a similar feel, with the fly theme very much to the fore. The top floor accommodates a vodka bar and plenty of chill-out space which is furnished with lots of comfy sofas. Music is integral to the lively atmosphere, and the DJ even gets his own pulpit beside the first floor bar. All great fun, but space is insufficient to cope with demand, so expect to queue.

THE FRONT PAGE   `13 J12`
106 Donegall Street Phone 324924
So called due to its location in the heart of the city's newspaper district, the Front Page is a busy upstairs bar which stages a live band several nights of the week - rock, folk and blues are all on offer.

THE GARRICK BAR   `14 K11`
29 Chichester Street Phone 321984
Beautifully preserved pub named after one of its for-mer patrons, David Garrick, a famous 18th century actor who used to pop in for a pint during rehearsals. Recent renovations have produced Back Stage at the Garrick, a nicely appointed dining room which caters to a steady stream of office workers and shoppers between noon and 6pm.

KAOS   `13 J9`
University Street
Nightclub, and popular student haunt, offering differ-

ent club nights every night of the week.

KELLY'S CELLARS `13 J11`
30 Bank Street
Phone 324835

Another city centre tavern steeped in history. The founding Kelly was Hugh who first got the drink flowing back in 1720. The stone-floored bar seems to have changed very little since it was used by Wolfe Tone and the United Irishmen to plan their 1798 Rebellion. Live traditional Irish music every Saturday, local bands are showcased every Friday night..

KING'S HEAD `20 G8`
829 Lisburn Road.
Phone 667805

The King's Head has managed to retain many original features from its former life as a Victorian mansion, including a civilised atmosphere. The layout is split into several rooms, one being a library lined with books should you happen to run out of conversation. A large conservatory has been added in recent years. Live music.

THE KITCHEN BAR `14 K11`
16 Victoria Square
Phone 324901

The sign outside reads,"City Drinking & Country Cooking", which sums things up pretty well, although it doesn't reveal the fact that this is a pub of two halves. The Kitchen Bar has changed very little since it opened in 1859, long and narrow, a bit of a man's bar, with horse racing on the TV, horse paintings over the bar, and punters busy nosebagging on an Ulster fry while debating the likely winner of this season's Premiership. Move on through to the Parlour Bar, however, and you can enjoy a bit more space and comfort. Live traditional Irish music on a regular basis.

LAVERY'S GIN PALACE `13 J9`
12 Bradbury Place.
Phone 327159

At the risk of over-using the word, Lavery's really is a Belfast institution. It's very popular with students, but all forms of life are here to behold, often packed in like sardines. Don't be surprised if you step inside only to find that you are making your way along the bar without your feet touching the floor. A good spot to study life, but not so good if you are looking for a quiet drink. The Back Bar is a popular venue for live music.

Robinsons - a pub crawl rolled into a single bar

THE LIMELIGHT & KATY DALY'S `13 J10`
17 Ormeau Avenue
Phone 325968

Bar and long established nightclub where the main focus is a diet of rock, funk and indie for the young and energetic! Club nights at the Limelight include Shag, a students' disco every Tuesday.

MAGENNIS'S `14 K10`
83 May Street. Phone 230295

Nobody can say that Magennis's hasn't moved with the times. A late 19th century bar, situated across the road from the Waterfront Hall and next door to the newly refurbished St George's Market, McGennis's is a hybrid of traditional and modern styles. Wooden snugs coexist comfortably with the new Whiskey Cafe which opts for a modern cafe bar look and serves a decent lunch for under a fiver. The menu reflects the decor - ranging from pasta and pesto to Irish stew. There are even a few tables outside and a couple of gas heaters to keep away the chill. The changes have been well received by many members of Belfast's in-crowd judging by the newfound popularity of the place, both during the day and long into the night.

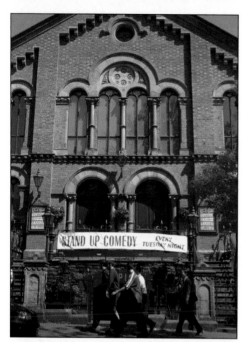

The Empire - comedy HQ and excellent live music venue

MANHATTAN `13 J9`
23 Bradbury Place
Phone 233131

Large, slightly brash, bar cum club, expensively fitted out with items of Americana. Caters to a younger crowd with resident DJ's every night of the week except for Sundays.

MERCURY `21 K8`
451 Ormeau Road
Phone 649017

The Ormeau Road has hardly been renowned over the years for being at the cutting edge of fashion but things are beginning to stir, and it's largely due the recent arrival of Mercury. Designer cool is the message, with acres of stainless steel, comfy velvet sofas, flat screen televisions hung like light fittings from the ceiling, and loads of natural light pouring in through the glass front and the pitched roof upstairs. There's even a glass water wall in the men's loo which makes your bladder an offer it simply can't refuse! Music is to the fore, and fans of Candid Camera might enjoy catching a glimpse of themselves on the video screens, while those of a shy disposition can at least be grateful for the fact that the loos are safe from the all seeing eye!

McHUGHS `14 K11`
29-31 Queen's Square.
Phone 249842

Belfast's thirty somethings are a fickle bunch who are inclined to transfer their loyalties at the drop of a Philip Treacy hat. McHughs is undoubtedly a trendy bar but when it opened a year or two ago in a slightly out of the way location, many predicted that the initial novelty value would quickly wear off and that the hordes of young professionals would soon migrate back to their traditional watering holes in and around the university area. McHughs seems to have lost little of its appeal, however, judging from the heaving masses which continue to pack the place out most nights of the week. The layout consists of a ground floor bar, downstairs club and upstairs restaurant, all nicely designed on an open plan with a strong emphasis on exposed brick and quirky fittings. The light fittings look as if they could give life to Frankenstein's monster but the most noteworthy item is a large chess set which is displayed in a glass cabinet at the back of the bar. The pieces have been modelled on various leading figures from Northern Ireland's over populated political world, and include such luminaries as Mo Mowlam, David Trimble, John Hulme, Gerry Adams and, of course, the big man himself, Ian Paisley.

McCAUSLAND HOTEL `14 K11`
34-38 Victoria Street. Phone 220200

The McCausland Building lay derelict for many years while awaiting redevelopment as part of the Laganside regeneration scheme. A four star hotel has provided the building with a new lease of life, with the added bonus of the Marco Polo Cafe Bar which provides comfort and style in which to enjoy a relaxing drink or a bite to eat.

MORNING STAR `14 K11`
17 Pottinger's Entry
Phone 323976

Hidden down a narrow alleyway, right in the heart of the city's main shopping district, the Morning Star is a listed building dating back to the early 18th century when it was a terminal for the Belfast to Dublin mail coach. Although very much a traditional pub, it is perhaps best known for its food, especially its Gourmet Nights which are held on the last Saturday of each month.

MORRISON'S `13 J10`
21 Bedford Street
Phone 248458

Morrison's may look old - it is themed on a turn of the

century spirit grocers - but it has been around for only a few years. Having replaced the Linen Hall (now closed) as a second home for some of the hacks from the BBC across the road, you may get to spot a few local celebs. Very popular bar which can get uncomfortably packed at weekends. Live music upstairs includes occasional Jazz and Blues.

NETWORK CLUB 13 J11
Lower North Street
Late night venue for serious clubbers who want to dance till dawn to sounds produced by heavyweight guest DJ's.

O'NEILL'S BAR 14 K11
4 Joy's Entry, off High Street
Phone 326711
O'Neill's is definitely not the kind of bar that you would expect to find when you venture up a narrow alleyway. The recent refurbishment has transformed it into a high ceilinged, spacious room, with a very contemporary feel. A smart place to lunch, and a forthcoming extension will even include a beer garden. Come Saturday night, the furniture is removed and O'Neills plays host to one of the most popular club nights in town.

PARLIAMENT BAR 14 K12
2 Dunbar Street
Phone 234520
The gay scene in Belfast has only begun to clamber out of the closet in recent years but the Parliament Bar has led the way with a daily menu of events. Weekend club nights go on until 7am. Other popular gay venues include the Kremlin at 96 Donegall Street.

PAT'S BAR 14 K12
19-22 Princes Dock Street
Phone 744524
Traditional dockside bar known for its friendly atmosphere and live traditional Irish music. Outdoor concerts on Clarendon Dock are a popular feature at weekends during the summer.

PAVILION BAR 21 K8
296-298 Ormeau Road
Phone 283283
Another Ormeau Road bar which has recently benefited from major refurbishment. The end result offers a large ground floor bar designed along traditional lines, an upstairs lounge which has pulled off the triple whammy of pine on the floor, walls *and* ceiling! The overall effect is slightly chintzy but the atmos-

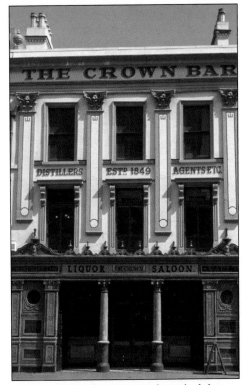

The Crown - Belfast's most treasured watering hole

phere is cosy and relaxed and a quite extensive wine list is on display if you reckon that a pint of the black stuff isn't sophisticated enough for your palate. And if relaxation isn't your cup of tea, there's even a disco on the top floor to complete the rather eclectic picture.

ROBINSON'S 13 J10
38 Great Victoria Street.
Phone 247447
The Troubles are hopefully over but their legacy lives on. Robinson's, which is situated almost next door to the Crown, had long been a Belfast landmark when it was burnt to the ground several years ago. Two million pounds later, it looks much as it did from the outside, but the inside has been reincarnated under various themes. The front bar has been painstakingly restored in keeping with the Victorian original but the back bar, now known as Fibber Magees, has been laid out as a 19th century general merchant's store. Go downstairs to the basement and you reach Rock Bottom, a bikers' bar complete with Harley Davidson. Even more themes feature throughout the other floors making it

Madisons - one of a new generation of Belfast cafe bars

possible to do a pub crawl without actually leaving Robinsons! On top of all that, there's a wide variety of live music and club nights on offer.

ROTTERDAM BAR `14 K12`
52-54 Pilot Street. Phone 753275
It doesn't look like much from the outside, and you might well wonder why you went a bit out of your way to get here, but the Rotterdam is currently one of the most unspoilt traditional style bars in Belfast. It occupies a fast changing world where it has recently been surrounded by brand new office developments and apartment blocks along Clarendon Dock. Open the door though and you immediately step back in time. A roaring fire, low ceilings and a tiled floor help to create a very convivial atmosphere. Live music, traditional, blues or rock, is on offer most nights of the week and outdoor concerts on the dockside are a regular weekend feature during the summer months.

RUMPOLE'S `14 K11`
81 Chichester Street. Phone 232840
Rumpole's is a pub with a bit of of a dual identity. As

its name might suggest, it is very close to the Law Courts and a popular watering hole with the legal fraternity, both at lunchtime and after work. By early evening the legal eagles are usually making other plans, however, and the pub reverts to the status of a 'local'.

SHENANAGAN ROOMS `13 J10`
21 Howard Street. Phone 323313
Previously the Washington Bar, the new theme is 'dyslexic Irish' judging by the spelling, with bare wood and stone dominating the interior. A wide cross section of customers populate the bar during the day, giving way to a younger crowd as night time approaches. Live music is a regular feature.

THOMPSONS GARAGE `13 J11`
Patterson's Place
Phone 323762
Situated down a quiet side street close to the City Hall this is an aptly named bar which rates a mention primarily for its popular club nights.

WELLINGTON PARK HOTEL `20 H7`
21 Malone Road. Phone 381111
The Welly Park, as it is affectionately known, is an institution which displays a split personality. Ostensibly, it is a very pleasant and comfortable hotel, recently extended, situated close to Queen's University. The foyer is so spacious that it's furnished with more comfy sofas than you'd expect to find at a branch of Sofaworld. There's even a grand piano to help promote the mellow atmosphere which prevails during the week. Come Friday and Saturday nights, however, the Welly is commandeered by a legion of Belfast's young (and not so young) professional types who like to end up here for a few late drinks to round off a good night's crack. Be prepared to listen to some dodgy chat up lines, but it's worth going just to see the face of the occasional hotel guest who checks in around midnight on their first trip to Belfast.

WHITE'S TAVERN `13 J11`
2-4 Winecellar Entry. Phone 243080
Belfast city centre has a few pubs which are hidden away down narrow alleyways but the nice thing about them is that you feel that you have unearthed a hidden jewel when you find them. White's fits firmly into this category, and the stone floors, exposed brickwork, low ceilings and the open fire give credence to the fact that thirsts have been satisfied here since 1630. Live traditional Irish music every Friday and Saturday.

Belfast has hundreds of restaurants and cafés to choose from but this guide attempts to select about 60 of the best. This process is bound to be subjective but no apologies are made for that. After all, how many times have you eaten at a restaurant for the first time because it happened to be recommended to you by somebody else?

All establishments featured have been tried out, often frequently, by somebody connected with the Belfast Street Atlas & Guide. They have been selected by people who enjoy good food and drink, bearing in mind price, location and diversity. These places are the ones that we have enjoyed most - the ones that we recommend to friends and relatives. They don't always agree, and perhaps you won't either, but that's what being subjective is all about! Having said that, we would be keen to hear your own recommendations or any objections that you might have regarding any of our choices.

What can be said, without fear of contradiction, is that the restaurant scene in Belfast has been transformed over the past ten years. Choice and quality have improved tremendously, and this trend looks set to continue. In terms of culinary diversity, price and atmosphere, Belfast restaurants can hold their own against most UK and Irish cities.

Many are mentioned in the growing array of good food guides. These publications all have their good points but, invariably, one area of contention is their attempts to estimate the likely cost of a meal. We have all had the experience of going somewhere supposedly "cheap & cheerful" only to find that a couple of drinks and a shared bottle of wine can do strange things to the bill. On the other hand, there are occasions when you may have taken advantage of a very reasonable fixed price menu, and left with both your conscience and the contents of your wallet largely intact!

When you add in lunchtime and early evening specials, fixed-price menus, and happy hours, attempts to estimate price often tend to be in vain. The system adopted for this guide, therefore, is rather broad-brush in its approach, attempting to categorise a restaurant as expensive, moderate or cheap.

"Expensive" restaurants are those where you can expect the final bill to exceed £25 per head. If you eat somewhere categorised as "cheap", you will, more often than not, escape for under a tenner. The final bill at a restaurant falling into the moderate category should fall somewhere between £10 and £25, bearing in mind all the caveats mentioned earlier.

Finally, the golden rule when using this guide is to phone first! All the information included was gathered in the summer of 1999, but restaurants come and go,

change ownership, chefs, menus, opening hours and much else, so it is best to check with the restaurant before turning up.

AERO   `13 J10`
44 Bedford Street. Phone 244844
Price Rating: ££
Aero occupies a site which was formerly home to Restaurant 44 and Bananas. In its new incarnation, style is very much the watch word. The opaque windows lend discretion to a warm, slightly minimilist, interior with light wooden floors, orange leather banquettes, canopied ceiling, tracked lighting, zinc bar, and unisex loos. The bold style statement extends to the menu which is ultra modern and cosmopolitan with a strong hint of Asian fusion. All in all, a very hip place to enjoy either lunch or dinner without breaking the bank. An early bird menu operates between 5.30pm and 7pm Monday to Friday, offering a good value opportunity to enjoy dinner for a tenner before heading out on the town. *Opening Times: Mon-Fri 12noon-2.30pm; Mon-Sat 5.30pm-10.30pm*

ALDEN'S   `15 Q10`
229 Upper Newtownards Road. Phone 650079
Price Rating: ££
The location may not suggest it, but Aldens can more than hold its own against Belfast's two better known heavyweights, Roscoff and Deanes. Serious foodies flock here to appreciate modern cooking served up in comfortable surroundings at affordable prices. *Opening Times: Mon-Sat 12noon-3pm & 6pm-10pm (11pm Fri & Sat); Sun 12noon-3pm*

ALTO'S   `13 J11`
6 Fountain Street. Phone 323087
Price Rating: £
Of the many cafes on Fountain Street this is perhaps the best, although the effort to impress is reflected in

Altos on Fountain Street

Sat 6.30pm-11pm

ASHOKA `20 G8`
363/365 Lisburn Road. Phone 660362
Price Rating: ££
It may look uninspiring from outside, but the Ashoka has been one of Belfast's most popular Indian restaurants for many years, offering a comprehensive menu which includes a good choice of vegetarian dishes and a few European alternatives. *Opening Times: Mon-Sat 5.30pm-11.30pm, sun 5.30pm-10.30pm*

THE BEAN `13 J11`
Royal Avenue
Espresso bar offering an excellent selection of coffees, although it's questionable as to whether there's a market in Belfast for iced coffee until global warming takes a firmer grip. A good choice of sandwiches and tray bakes is complimented by a few hot options from the specials board. The small, but ultra modern layout provides extra seating upstairs where you can sit and watch the world go by as you graze.

BEATRICE KENNEDY'S `13 J9`
44 University Road. Phone 202290
Price Rating: ££
Intimate restaurant named after the lady who used to live here before it became an eaterie. The dining room retains much of the period feel of the house and the menu tends to stick to solid and dependable favourites which keep the customers coming back for more. *Opening Times: Mon-Sun 5pm-10.30pm*

BELFAST CASTLE `6 H18`
Antrim Road
Phone 776925
Price Rating : ££
The Cellar Restaurant is situated in the basement of this Belfast landmark which was formerly home to the Marquis of Donegall. What better way to digest lunch or dinner than to stroll to the top of Cave Hill and enjoy the spectacular view over Belfast. Sunday lunch is served upstairs in the Ben Madigan Restaurant. *Opening Times: Mon-Sat 11am-2.30pm & 6.30pm-9.45pm; Sun 12noon-2.30pm*

BENGAL BRASSERIE `21 K8`
339 Ormeau Road.
Phone 647516
Price Rating : ££
Highly rated Bengali cooking which includes a list of daily specials such as Tandoori Duck and Indian River Fish. *Opening Times: Mon-Sat 12noon-2pm & 5.30pm-11.15pm; Sun 5.30pm-10.15pm*

the price. The dining room is cool and airy with a high ceiling and modern art adorning the walls. The menu doesn't stay the same for long but it's normally innovative and tends to reflect a strong Mediteranean influence. Forget your bangers and mash - it's Toulouse sausage in these parts, and be prepared to pay a five or six quid for the privilege, although it's well worth it. A decent selection of wines and a few outside tables are an added bonus. *Opening Times: Mon-Sat 10pm-6pm; Thurs-Sat 7pm-10.30pm*

ANTICA ROMA `13 J9`
67 Botanic Avenue. Phone 311121
Price Rating : £££
Antica Roma takes a step up market from its sister restaurants, Speranza and Villa Italia, but there is still a strong emphasis on having a fun night out. Most notable, is the decor which, in its efforts to capture the mood of ancient Rome, successfully conveys what it must be like to eat on the movie set of a Hollywood epic. The food receives mixed reports but it still rates a mention in most of the good food guides. The atmosphere is lively, especially at weekends and, all in all, Antica Roma remains a fashionable place to see and be seen. *Opening Times: Mon-Fri 12noon-2.30pm; Mon-*

BISHOPS `13 J9`
34 Bradbury Place. Price Rating: £
Arguably the best fish and chip shop in Belfast, with an excellent choice of fresh fish, and plenty of alternatives which include burgers, chicken and even a few vegetarian options. A spacious and comfortable seating area is provided should you choose to dine in. *Opening Times: Mon-Sun 11am-3am*

BONNIE'S MUSEUM CAFE `20 J7`
11a Stranmillis Road. Phone 663266
Price Rating: £
Situated just across the road from the Ulster Museum and the Botanic Gardens, this very attractive dining space previously served as a studio to the famous Belfast artist, William Conor. The lofty ceiling and abundance of natual light are compimented by brightly coloured walls which are lined with modern art. You can dine for a fiver from an extensive lunch menu which is available between 12noon and 7pm. Evening diners select from a shorter, but no less interesting, bistro menu. *Opening Times: Mon-Thurs 9am-11pm; Fri-Sun 9am-1.30am*

CAFE POIROT `13 J11`
51 Fountain Street. Phone 323130
Price Rating: £
French-style cafe offering a good range of fresh sandwiches and light meals which have been very popular with hungry shoppers and office workers for many years. Fountain Street can be a good sun trap and so an outside table can be a relaxing way to spend your lunchtime, queues and weather permitting! *Opening Times: Mon-Sat 7.45am-5.30pm (until 7.30pm Thurs)*

CAFE RENOIR `13 J11`
5 Queen Street. Phone 325592
Price Rating: £
Ever popular lunchtime haunt for shoppers and nearby office workers. Has had a bit of a face lift recently but the look remains bright and welcoming. The menu board offers modern and interesting options which means that it normally pays to arrive early for lunch. *Opening Times: Mon-Sat 9.45am-5pm*

CAFE SOCIETY `13 J11`
3 Donegall Square East. Phone 439525
Price Rating: ££
Downstairs bistro and slightly more formal resturant upstairs where you can enjoy a view over the City Hall gardens. Good food complimented by an excellent wine list. Resident pianist, and live Jazz at 5pm on Friday afternoons. *Opening Times: Mon-Sat 8am until late*

Beatrice Kennedy's on University Road

CARGOES `20 G8`
613 Lisburn Road. Phone 665451
Price Rating: £
Very trendy cafe and delicatessen serving morning coffee, lunch and afternoon tea from a menu which changes on a daily basis, but always includes a good choice of salads, salami and cheeses. If you are an American, suffering withdrawal symptoms for the want of waffles and maple syrup, this is the place to come for Sunday brunch. Opening Times: Mon-Sat 9pm-5pm; Sun 9.30am-4.30pm

CHEZ DELBART `13 J9`
10 Bradbury Place.
Phone 238020
Price Rating: ££
Known locally as Frogities, this was a popular resturant back in the days before the term 'Belfast's Golden Mile' had even been coined. Its popularity shows no sign of abating which says much for the authentic bistro food and atmosphere conjured up within. *Opening Times: Tues-Sat 5pm-12midnight; Sun5pm-9.30pm*

CUTTERS WHARF `20 J6`
Lockview Road. Phone 663388
Price Rating : ££
The restaurant, like the bar below, has a boathouse feel to it which fits in nicely with its riverside location. The menu offers a good range of modern European cuisine and the service is efficient and friendly. And if you enjoy a drink or two before or after dinner, the bar downstairs is one of the busiests in Belfast. Opening Times: Mon-Fri 12noon-10.30pm; Sat 6pm-10.30pm

DEANE'S `13 J10`
38 Howard Street. Phone 560000
Price Rating: £££
Michael Deane has been in the restaurant business for many years but, since moving from Helen's Bay to Howard Street, he has truly entered the limelight and acquired a Michelin Star along the way. Deane's is divided between a downstirs brasserie, where the atmosphere is lively and relaxed, and the restaurant upstairs where the cooking is even more adventurous but the atmosphere a little more corporate. *Opening Times: Brasserie Mon-Sat 12noon-3pm & 5pm-11pm; Restaurant Tues-Fri 7pm-9.30pm*

DRAGON PALACE `13 J9`
16 Botanic Avenue. Phone 323869
Price Rating : ££
One of the busiest Chinese restaurants in town offering a popular combination of good food and reasonable prices. *Opening Times: Mon-Sun 12noon-2pm & 5pm-12midnight*

THE EDGE `14 L11`
Mays Meadow. Phone 322000
Price Rating: £££
The Bank Gallery Restaurant is located on the first floor of this three storey £2m complex which has recently opened on the banks of the river, just behind the Waterfront Hall. It is difficult to judge at this early juncture, but the Edge will do well to develop the buzz enjoyed by some of its more centrally located rivals. The menu relies on mostly familiar offerings but the food is well cooked and presented and the staff are very attentive.

EQUINOX `13 J10`
32 Howard Street
Price Rating: £
Equinox is best known as a shop where discerning brides leave their wedding list so that they can stock up on Alessi, and other such brands of kitchen and dinner ware, at somebody else's expense! The small cafe area at the back is an additional treat where you can select from a goat's cheese and olive type menu and dine off a Rosenthal plate. The desserts are difficult to resist, the prices are very keen, and all in all it's a top notch place to have lunch or a daytime coffee. *Opening Times: Mon-Sat 9.30am-4.45pm*

FEASTS `13 J10`
Dublin Road
Why stop at opening a trendy new coffee bar when, like Feasts, you can throw in a delicatessen and fromagerie for good measure!

GREEN'S PIZZERIA `20 G8`
549 Lisburn Road. Phone 666033
Price Rating: £
A popular spot due to its attractive, exposed brick and pine interior and excellent pizzas. Bring your own booze, and no booking, are policies of the house, but should you find yourself facing a lengthy wait for a table, you can request a bleeper and retire across the road for an aperitif at the Chelsea

HAAGEN-DAZS `20 G8`
Lisburn Road
One look at the sleek layout, beech and blue velvet to the fore, should be enough to forewarn you that you are about to part with four quid for a portion of ice cream. But Häagen-Dazs do know a thing or two about making delicious ice cream, and we all deserve a little indulgence now and then. Coffeee and nibbles are also availble.

HARRY RAMSDEN'S `9 K13`
Yorkgate Shopping Centre. Phone 749222
Price Rating: £
Part of a chain offering 'the most famous fish and chips in the world', from Yorksire to Hong Kong, Melbourne, and now Belfast. The restaurant is large, comfortable, and licensed, the fish and chips live up to their billing, and there are even a few alternatives to choose from if you prefer meat. *Opening Times: Mon-Thurs 11.30am-10.30pm; Fri & Sat 11.30am-11pm; Sun 12.30pm-10.30pm*

JHARNA `20 G8`
133 Lisburn Road.
Phone 381299
Price Rating: ££
Attractive, Indian restaurant with a good reputation for seafood dishes (the Fish Badami is so good that somebody in England once placed a take away order and had it flown to Bournemouth at a cost of £1500). *Opening Times: Mon-Sat 12noon-2pm & 5.30pm-11.30pm; Sun 5.30pm-11pm*

LA BELLE EPOQUE `13 J10`
61-63 Dublin Road. Phone 323244
Price Rating: £££
Heavyweight French restaurant which is popular with diners who like to combine business with pleasure. The atmosphere is a little bit formal but still manages to remain relaxed, while the food is good enough to rate a mention in most of the good food guides. The fixed price lunch and dinner menus offer good value and may help to limit the damage when the bill arrives. *Opening Times: Mon-Fri 12noon-11pm; Sat 6pm-11pm*

LA SALSA MEXICAN RESTAURANT `13 J9`
23 University Road. Phone 244588
Price Rating: £
Belfast seems to be acquiring the taste for Mexican food but, if the chillies prove too hot at La Salsa, you can always douse the flames with a frozen margarita or three. Mariachi music to the fore and live flamenco guitar every Wednesday downstairs. *Opening Times: Mon-Sun 5pm-11pm*

LARRY'S `13 J10`
36 Bedford Street. Phone 325061
Price Rating: ££
There's nothing formal about the atmosphere at Larry's which is a popular choice if you are going out in a group and want to let your hair down a bit. The piano gets plenty of use and it is not unknown for the staff to do a turn. Don't be surprised to see dancing on the table or the occasional body sliding under it. Last orders 1.15am.

LAZIZ `13 J9`
99 Botanic Avenue. Phone 233666
Price Rating: ££
Tastefully appointed Moroccan restaurant which deserves to succeed, although only time will tell whether there's sufficient demand from Belfast diners for north African cuisine, much of which is cooked in traditional clay pots.

MALONEY'S `20 H7`
33/35 Malone Road. Phone 682929
Price Rating : ££
Long established restaurant, frequented by local residents, which helps to promote a warm and friendly atmosphere. Menu is varied, with a mixture of continental and traditional cooking. *Opening Times: Mon-Sat 12noon-11pm; Sun 12noon-10pm*

MANGETOUS `13 J9`
30 University Road. Phone 222722

Mangetous on University Road

Price Rating: ££
Simple but attractive cafe cum bistro situated right in the heart of the university area. Coffee, croissants and snacks are served all day, a 2 course lunch special is available for a fiver, and an interesting dinner menu offers something more substantial as the evening approaches. *Opening Times: Mon-Sat 11am-11pm; Sun 12.30pm-10pm*

MANOR HOUSE `13 J9`
47 Donegall Pass. Phone 238755
Price Rating : ££
At first glance, a traditional Chinese restaurant but the menu reveals a few surprises that help the Manor House to stand out from the pack. Fish head, duck's web, eel - all cooked in an authentic Cantonese style which has brought the restaurant to the attention of most of the good food guides. Good value set menus both at lunch and dinner, and an excellent selection of vegetarian dishes. *Opening Times: Mon-Sat 12noon-2.30pm & 5pm-11.30pm; Sun 12.30pm-11pm*

NICK'S WAREHOUSE `14 K12`
35-39 Hill Street. Phone 439690
Price Rating: ££
Restaurant and wine bar situated in what used to be a rather unfashionable part of town near to St Anne's Cathedral. Nick's pioneering spirit has been rewarded with a large and loyal following, especially among the business community who have made this one of the most popular places in town both at lunchtime and in the evening. A recent extension of the downstirs wine bar into the building next door has helped to satisfy demand but there's still a good buzz throughout. The food is cooked with a certain zest which earns it an enthusiastic reception from both customers and food critics alike. *Opening Times: Mon-Fri 12noon-3pm; Tues-Sat 6pm-11pm*

OPUS ONE `13 J9`
1 University Street, Belfast 7. Phone 590101
Price Rating: ££
New restaurant development on the site of the former Saints & Scolars and Aubergines & Blue Jeans. This is a big budget affair, laid out on different levels, with seating for up to 200 diners . The interior is designed on an art deco theme, but the newness of it all rather undermines the attempt to conjure up a bygone era. The cuisine, which is French, and the service are both top notch, however, and should be enough to ensure that Opus One will enjoy broad appeal. Open for lunch and dinner 7 days a week. Live entertainment is a regular feature.

THE OTHER PLACE `20 J7`
133 Stranmillis Road. Phone 207100
Price Rating: £
Cafe style dining and a lively atmosphere, all day long, which has gone down well in south Belfast judging by the opening of two other brances on Botanic Avenue and the Lisburn Road. All three outlets are popular, both as places to eat and as somewhere to relax with a good cup of coffee. Unlicensed.

PIZZA EXPRESS `13 J10`
25-27 Dublin Road.
Phone 329050
Price Rating: £
Relative newcomer to Belfast, but the formula is the same as in the rest of the UK and Ireland - good location, stylish, open-plan interior, friendly service, and arguably the best pizzas in town, although alernatives are limited to a couple of pasta dishes and a couple of salads. Can be very busy but it's usually worth the wait. A no booking policy is the norm except for large groups. *Opening Times: Mon-Sun 11.30am-11pm*

PLANET HARVEYS `13 J10`
95 Great Victoria Street. Phone 233433
Price Rating: ££
American style diner serving a wide-ranging menu which includes plenty of pizzas, pasta, burgers and Tex Mex options.

PLANKS `20 G8`
479-481 Lisburn Road. Phone 663211
Price Rating: ££
Some restaurants inadvertently resemble a building site but at Planks the look is intentioal. Good value food, friendly service, and a bring your own wine policy, attracts a lively young crowd. Open for breakfast, lunch and dinner.

REVELATIONS INTERNET CAFE `13 J9`
27 Shaftesbury Square
Surf the web for £5 an hour and, if you have any money left, treat yourself to a decent cup of coffee and a gourmet sandwich. *Opening Times: Mon-Fri 10pm-8pm; Sun 12noon-8pm*

ROSCOFF `13 J9`
Lesley House, Shaftesbury Square. Phone 331532
Price Rating: £££
It was Mark Twain who once remarked that reports of his death were greatly exaggerated. So it is with Roscoff, which may have losts its Michelin Star in 1999, but TV chefs Paul and Jeanne Rankin's restaurant is still at, or very near, the top of the pile when it comes to eating out in Belfast. From outside, the premises could be mistaken for a bookmaker's shop, but behind its opaque windows the decor is light and modern, the cooking is always creative, and the menu is constantly changing. Fixed price lunch and dinner menus for just under £20 and £30 respectively, may not be cheap, but the expreience is usually worth it, especially when Paul Rankin is in the kitchen. *Opening Times: Mon-Fri 12.15pm-2.15pm; Mon-Sat 6.30pm-10.30pm*

ROSCOFF CAFE & BAKERY `13 J11`
27-29 Fountain Street. Phone 315090
Price Rating: £
Smallest of the three Roscoff outlets which caters mainly to hungry and foot-sore shoppers. Breakfast is served until 11am, but a gourmet sandwich and/or a mouth watering pastry tends to be a more popular option, normally washed down with the help of a giant cup of cappuccino. *Opening Times: Mon-Sat 7.30am-5.30pm (until 8.30pm Fri & Sat)*

ROSCOFF CAFE EXPRESS `13 K11`

Upper Arthur Street.
Price Rating: £
The latest addition to the Roscoff empire, this branch is bigger and more comfortable than its sister cafe on Fountain Street. The look and feel are familiar - fashion conscious clientele, here to enjoy modern, simple cooking which utilises only the best fresh ingredients. There are a few outside tables when the weather permits and a take away service is on offer if you haven't got time to linger.

RUBY TUESDAY'S `20 G8`
629 Lisburn Road
Phone 661220
Price Rating: £
Part of an expanding empire with other branches on the Stranmillis Road (phone 667419) and the Antrim Road. A very popular venue for breakfast at weekends, Ruby Tuesdays evolves from cafe during the day to restaurant by nightfall, when diners choose from a bistro type menu. *Opening Times: Mon-Sun 7.45am until late.*

SHANKS
Blackwood Golf Centre, Crawfordsburn Rd, Bangor
Phone (01247) 853313
Price Rating: £££
Please don't ask what a restaurant of this name is doing at a golf centre. Shanks is situated about 20 minutes by car out of Belfast, but the detour is well worth it for this Michelin Star establishment which overlooks rolling countryside. The dining room was designed by Sir Terence Conran, but customers come primarily for the cooking and service provided by husband and wife team, Robbie and Shirley Millar. *Opening Times: Tues-Sat 12noon-2pm & 7pm-10.30pm; Sun 12noon-2pm; Mon 12.30pm-4pm*

THE SKANDIA `13 J10`
50 Howard Street.
Phone 240239
Price Rating: ££
Howard Street is one of several outlets in the Skandia empire which, although not a name readily associated with trendy eating, has survived and thrived for decades as others have come and gone. Menus change according to whether its morning, noon or night but the emphasis is on straight forward cooking, good value, and a family atmosphere. Although unlicensed, you are welcome to bring your own wine. The nearby Callender Street branch is located in the heart of the city's shopping district and stays open during retail hours.

Roscoff Cafe & Bakery on sunny Fountain Street

SPERANZA `13 J9`
16/17 Shaftesbury Square. Phone 230213
Price Rating: £
Although a bit easier on the pocket than her sister restaurants, Villa Italia and Antica Roma, the family likeness remains. A large bustling restaurant which operates a no-booking policy, Speranza concentrates primarily on pizzas and pasta. The atmosphere is lively and informal, and children are made welcome. *Mon-Sat 5.30pm-11.30pm; Sun 5.30pm-10.30pm*

THE SQUARE `13 J10`
89 Dublin Road. Phone 239933
Price Rating: ££
Relative newcomer which manages to attract a lively crowd both upstairs and down. The a la carte menu does't stay the same for long but an interesting choice of modern international cuisine is usually on offer alongide a choice of daily specials. *Opening Times: Mon-Sat 10am-10.30pm*

THE STRAND `20 J7`
12 Stranmillis Road. Phone 682266
Price Rating: ££
The Strand places a strong emphasis on quality which

Be prepared to queue at ever-popular Villa Italia

helps to explain why it has remained one of Belfast's more popular restaurants for so long. The menu is wide ranging and ever changing - food is served throughout the day and there are plenty of special options such as the speciality breakfasts at the weekend, fixed price Sunday lunch, and a gourmet menu on the last Wednesday of each month. Opening Times: Mon-Sun 12noon -11pm

THE STREAT `13 J10`
79 Dublin Road. Phone 236919. Fax 329343
Good coffee and an extensive range of freshly made sandwiches are available to take away from this bright and modern coffee bar, but why not grab a high stool at the counter and enjoy the comings and goings while you sip your cappuccino and contemplate the rest of the day. If you are chained to an office desk for your sins, you can always fax your order before 11am and have it delivered by lunctime.

THE SUN KEE `13 J9`
38 Donegall Pass. Phone 312016
Price Rating: ££
From the outside, the Sun Kee has the look of a place that has been shut for several years, but diners are

drawn here for the authenticity of the food which is reckoned by many to be the best Chinese nosh in town. The dining space is one simple room where you bring along your own wine and beer and enjoy the friendly service and relaxed atmosphere. *Mon-Sun 5pm-11pm*

SUWANNA `13 J10`
Great Victoria Street. Price Rating: ££
Cafe style restaurant serving delicious Thai cuisine. Bring your own bottle.

TAJ MAHAL `13 J9`
96 Botanic Avenue. Phone 313999
Price Rating: ££
Large Indian restaurant serving a wide range of dishes in comfortable surroundings. The three course business lunch at £4.95 offers exceptional value.

TEDFORDS RESTAURANT `14 K11`
5 Donegall Quay. Phone 434000
Price Rating: £££
Fish restaurant located on the banks of the river overlooking the Lagan Weir. The choice of fish is extensive although a little bit expensive, but the end product is invariably fresh and beautifully prepared. Tedfords may be a little bit out of the way but this area is on the up and, if you fancy a drink before or after your meal, a short stroll around the corner will bring you to either McHughs or McCauslands where you can enjoy a post prandial tipple in some style. *Opening Times: Mon-Fri 12noon-3pm; Tues-Sat 6pm-10.30pm*

VILLA ITALIA `13 J9`
39/41 University Road. Price Rating: ££
Villa Italia has taught Belfast quite a bit about the art of queuing over the years, but its popularity remains undimmed despite a no-booking policy and increasing competition from new outlets nearby. Its success is based on a formula of reasonably priced Italian food served by attractive staff in one of the livliest spots in town. *Opening Times : Mon-Fri 5.30pm-11.30pm; Sat 4pm-11.30pm; Sun 4pm-10.30pm*

THE WELCOME `20 J7`
22 Stranmillis Road. Phone 381359
Price Rating : ££
With a pagoda roof over the entrance and an abundance of dragons, screens and lanterns inside, there is no mistaking this Welcome for anything other than a Chinese one. Established more than 25 years ago, the highly rated cooking is a combination of Cantonese, Pekinese and Szechwan and the choice of dishes is exhaustive. *Opening Times: Mon-Sat 12noon-2pm & 5pm-11.30pm; Sun 5pm-10.30pm*